Tragic Design

The Impact of Bad Product Design and How to Fix It

Jonathan Shariat and Cynthia Savard Saucier

 Beijing · Boston · Farnham · Sebastopol · Tokyo

Tragic Design
by Jonathan Shariat and Cynthia Savard Saucier

Published by O'Reilly Media, Inc., 1005 Gravenstein Highway North, Sebastopol, CA 95472.

O'Reilly books may be purchased for educational, business, or sales promotional use. Online editions are also available for most titles (http://oreilly.com/safari). For more information, contact our corporate/institutional sales department: (800) 998-9938 or corporate@oreilly.com.

Acquisitions Editor: Mary Treseler
Editor: Angela Rufino
Production Editor: Nicholas Adams
Copyeditor: Rachel Head
Proofreader: Molly Ives Brower

Indexer: Lucie Haskins
Cover Designer: Randy Comer
Interior Designers: Ron Bilodeau and Monica Kamsvaag
Illustrator: Rebecca Demarest
Compositor: Nicholas Adams

April 2017: First Edition.

Revision History for the First Edition:

    2017-04-07   First release

See http://oreilly.com/catalog/errata.csp?isbn=0636920038887 for release details.

978-1-491-92361-0

[LSI]

[*contents*]

Foreword

Much of what Shariat and Savard Saucier write in this book, I might not have fully understood at all if I'd never left the academy. Leaving wonderful places like MIT and RISD to join the world of industry isn't what good, pure "thought leaders" normally do, but all of my interactions with the new kinds of designers emerging in the technology industry made me think my thoughts weren't really good enough anymore. So I've been busy filling up my brain with the many new experiences that I've gained by working in Silicon Valley at a thankfully late stage in my career. I say this with gratitude because I would have hated to have lived my entire life in the untouchable Ivory Tower without knowing what I do today. What have I learned about the future in Silicon Valley working in venture capital and advising technology companies? That the impact of Moore's Law—the doubling of computing power every 18 months—is still making its way to people around the world. But the mitigating factor for technology's real impact in people's lives isn't a technical one of speed, scale, or power. It isn't a matter measured in gigahertz, terabytes, or nanopixels—it is instead the pursuit of satisfying human needs for comprehensibility, ease of use, and emotional fit in our digital experiences today. It is a matter of purposefully designing superior solutions with technology that can empower and support humans.

Where are the designers for these new directions to be found? I find that a lot of them are in the startup community—specifically, in companies whose CEOs and cofounders lead their ventures with a designer's penchant for disrupting the status quo while centering their businesses' objectives around what people want and need, rather than solely what new technologies can make possible. They are people like designers Brian Chesky and Joe Gebbia, who reframed the hospitality industry (*https://www.airbnb.com*) as a distributed network of bedrooms in people's own houses to rent like hotel rooms. Or the nondesigner

CEOs of public companies like John Donahoe, who formerly led eBay Inc. to adopt design thinking at the executive level across his companies. Or people like Marissa Vosper and Lauren Schwab, cofounders of tiny New York–based apparel startup Negative Underwear (*https://negativeunderwear.com*), where technical fabrics are used to achieve fit and aesthetic needs that male lingerie designers have long overlooked. If you would like to learn more about this phenomenon, just look at the Design in Tech Reports (*http://DesignIn.Tech*) from the past three years; you'll see that the impact of design in the technology industry is truly growing.

But with great impact comes great failures too. The many tragedies described in this book are evident throughout the technology industry, and to see them summarized in the way that Shariat and Savard Saucier present them is truly disheartening. And unfortunately, because of the way that the design profession is taught in the academy today, driven primarily by aesthetics and in the absence of testing or other data gathering, we'll likely see even more tragedies introduced through our apps, screens, and assorted IoT devices. For that reason, this book appears at an opportune time to encourage designers of all skill levels to break their honed Bauhausian biases, abandon their fine-tuned taste-o-meters, and bridge a path to the kind of vital, tragedy-preventing design that Shariat and Savard Saucier propose. I feel lucky that I get to put many of these principles into practice at Automattic (*https://automattic.com*).

What does design have to do with "inclusion"? I think that will become fully evident as you read through this book. Digital technology used to be available only to "computer nerds"—but now, because of smartphones, digital technology is accessible to everyone. So it now needs to be considered from an inclusive viewpoint, encompassing the full variety of human beings that live on this planet, and not just highly skilled computer types. This revolution is just beginning, and it's exciting to have Shariat and Savard Saucier's book to ground the growing movement of achieving truly inclusive design in the digital era.

John Maeda is Global Head of Computational Design and Inclusion at Automattic Inc. He is a Strategic Advisor to venture capital firm Kleiner Perkins Caufield & Byers, has led research teams at the MIT Media Lab, and was the 16th president of the Rhode Island School of Design. His work is represented in the permanent collection of the Museum of Modern Art.

Preface

BAD DESIGN DECISIONS CAN HARM. However, the designers making these decisions aren't always aware of the responsibilities that come with their profession.

In medical school, the first fundamental principle that students are taught is *Primum non nocere*, or in plain English, "First, do no harm." This immediately reinforces the concept that physicians have a lot of power over a person's life. In contrast, the first thing we were taught in design school was how to draw well in 3D perspective. Our teachers were obsessed with timeless and beautiful designs. We would strive for polished design and were greatly concerned by aesthetic qualities. Accordingly, we were rewarded for following trends and using appealing color palettes. Very rarely were we reminded that we have responsibilities and that what we design has a real impact on people's lives.

If we were lucky, we had a single three-hour-long class on user experience...and the teacher probably called this a "Human–Computer Interaction" class. For example, in four years at university, neither Cynthia nor Jonathan was required to observe a single user interacting with a product they had designed!

After school, new designers carefully select the best projects they've realized and put them into a portfolio. The rest, the bad and potentially dangerous projects, are dumped in an "archive" folder with the hope that no one will ever find it. If you're like us, you are so ashamed by some of these solutions that you might even rename this folder to something completely unrelated, to make sure that no one ever sees it, even by mistake. Fortunately, this bad design work is forgotten and forgiven! Not a single user will ever have to deal with the consequences of the questionable design decisions that we made as students.

But by focusing on the beauty scale, and allowing for any mistakes to blissfully disappear into an archive folder, our teachers and mentors neglect to address what's worse than getting a C– in a class. What actually happens with failing projects in the real world? What can we learn from our mistakes, while the consequences of our inexperience are still trivial? We should be taught that, as designers, we have a lot of power to influence the way users interact with our products. And, to quote Spider-Man's uncle: *with great power comes great responsibility.*

Our teachers are not the only ones to blame. When is the last time you wondered if your work might have killed someone? This book wants to make sure no designer ever signs off on work without considering the consequences of their decisions. We want to give you tools and techniques, applicable in a real-life context, that will enable you to make fair decisions in difficult situations.

Humans are complex beings with the capability of feeling a huge range of emotions. "Designing with empathy" is a trendy concept. There are a multitude of books, articles, and even design firms focused on this subject. But what does that even mean? What emotions are we really designing for? As designers, developers, and product creators, we selectively choose which emotions to design for and which to ignore. We may *say* that we apply a user-centered design methodology, but often we don't even get to talk with a single user before launching our product. The experiences we create affect *real people* in *real situations.* Unfortunately, it is not as popular to discuss and debate the responsibilities that come with the great power that we are entrusted with.

We should learn from disciplines outside of our own. For example, in Canada and some places in the US, graduating engineers have a ritual of receiving an iron ring during their graduation ceremony. But what's the story behind this ring?

In the 1900s, during the construction of the Quebec Bridge, it collapsed, killing 75 people. The collapse was due to an error in judgment by the engineers who designed the bridge. There's a myth that says the first rings were made from the iron of the collapsed bridge to symbolize humility and to serve as a reminder of their obligation, ethic, and responsibility to the public.

Graduating designers aren't given rings. This book is an attempt at filling that gap. This book is a call to action for everyone to find their own ring.

About This Book

This book explores the types of harm that can result from what we consider "bad" design. As you will learn, design can *kill* (Chapters 1 and 2), can *anger* (Chapter 3), can *sadden* (Chapter 4), and can *exclude* people (Chapter 5). Fortunately there are tools and techniques to prevent causing this harm, and there are many groups, companies, and organizations already helping to make the world a better place. These chapters present examples of bad design and the negative outcomes of these, followed by key learnings. All the chapters end with interviews with leaders who are recognized as authorities in their fields. They were generous with their knowledge and advice, and we hope they contribute to broadening your perspective on the subject of design. You will also find some personal stories on how bad design has had a negative impact, told by the designers who lived them. We appreciate how difficult telling these deeply personal stories must have been, and we hope that they will serve as inspiration for you.

Finally, in the last three chapters of the book we will offer some techniques and activities that can help designers to prevent causing harm unintentionally. We then offer options of things you can do to help and highlight some companies that are already doing amazing work.

O'Reilly Safari

Safari (formerly Safari Books Online) is a membership-based training and reference platform for enterprise, government, educators, and individuals.

Members have access to thousands of books, training videos, Learning Paths, interactive tutorials, and curated playlists from over 250 publishers, including O'Reilly Media, Harvard Business Review, Prentice Hall Professional, Addison-Wesley Professional, Microsoft Press, Sams, Que, Peachpit Press, Adobe, Focal Press, Cisco Press, John Wiley & Sons, Syngress, Morgan Kaufmann, IBM Redbooks, Packt, Adobe Press, FT Press, Apress, Manning, New Riders, McGraw-Hill, Jones & Bartlett, and Course Technology, among others.

For more information, please visit *http://oreilly.com/safari*.

Comments and Questions

Please address comments and questions concerning this book to the publisher:

O'Reilly Media, Inc.

1005 Gravenstein Highway North

Sebastopol, CA 95472

(800) 998-9938 (in the United States or Canada)

(707) 829-0515 (international or local)

(707) 829-0104 (fax)

We have a web page for this book, where we list errata, examples, and any additional information. You can access this page at: *http://bit.ly/ tragic-design*. The authors have set up a website for the book as well at *http://www.tragicdesign.com*.

To comment or ask technical questions about this book, send email to *bookquestions@oreilly.com*.

For more information about our books, courses, conferences, and news, see our website at *http://www.oreilly.com*.

Find us on Facebook: *http://facebook.com/oreilly*

Follow us on Twitter: *http://twitter.com/oreillymedia*

Watch us on YouTube: *http://www.youtube.com/oreillymedia*

Acknowledgments

Jonathan

To my everything, my wife Forouzan. Not only was it you that shared with me your teacher's story of Jenny, which sparked the heart of this book, but you have supported me through all the highs and lows of this journey.

To my coauthor Cynthia, this book wouldn't be half of what it is without your hard work and vast knowledge. *Merci beaucoup!*

Thanks also to my friends Sam Mazaheri, Chris Liu, and my mentor Andy Law, who have helped shape me into a better designer and person; to Eric Meyer and Jared Spool, who provided critical guidance to me early on; and to all the people along the way who went out of their way to help us. I've been deeply touched by the support and kindness of the global design community.

Lastly, to Shawn Chittle, whose tweet to Tim O'Reilly made this happen, and to Tim, who took a chance on me: thank you for the honor of being able to bring light to these important issues.

Cynthia

To my son, Émile, who spent countless hours sleeping on my knees while I wrote this book and teaches me to be the best version of myself, *je t'aime Poupou.*

To my fiancé, Mathieu, who has heard the story of "How I stabbed my friend" a thousand times, *merci* Chicken.

This book would not exist if my friend Fred hadn't almost died. Thank you for not dying that day.

To my coauthor, Jonathan, for hearing my feedback and inviting me to join this project, I owe you one!

To our editor, Angela, for your time, feedback, and patience, thanks.

To all of our contributors, reviewers, helpers, and those who allowed us to use their images, resources, ideas, and words, thank you for your generosity.

Introduction

The Interface that Killed Jenny

Stories of deaths caused by badly designed interfaces, objects, or experiences are everywhere. One, in particular, inspired us to write this book.

Jenny, as we will call her, was a young girl diagnosed with cancer. She was in and out of the hospital for a number of years, then was finally discharged. A while later she relapsed and had to start a new treatment with very potent medicine. This treatment was so aggressive that it required pre-hydration and post-hydration for three days through intravenous fluids. After the medicine was administered, the nurses were to be responsible for entering all the required information into the charting software and using this software to follow up on the patient's status and make appropriate interventions.

Although the attending nurses used the software diligently, and even though they cared very well for Jenny in every other way, they missed the critical information about her three-day hydration requirements.

The day after her treatment, Jenny died of toxicity and dehydration.

The experienced nurses made this critical error because they were too distracted trying to figure out the software. Looking at screenshots (see Figure 1-1) of the software they used is infuriating. It violates so many simple and basic rules of usability, it is no wonder why the nurses were distracted. First, the density of information is so high that it's impossible to scan for critical information quickly. Second, the colors selected, aside from being further distracting, prevent any critical information from being highlighted. Third, any critical treatment or drug information should receive special treatment so it is not missed, which is not what we see in this interface. Lastly, the flow of recording the information after each visit, known as "charting," requires too much time and attention to complete in a timely manner.

FIGURE 1-1.

A screenshot of the Epic charting software used by many hospitals in the US (source: *http://www.clientscorner.com/informaticslearning/scenario01.php*)

As design professionals, learning about these stories is heart-wrenching. How can a critical, life-or-death service be employing such horrible software? Isn't a person's life and well-being worth putting the appropriate resources into good design? It's almost impossible not to ask ourselves if we could have made a difference in preventing Jenny's death, had we been involved in the design process.

Healthcare in the United States is facing a crisis. In 1999 a landmark report titled "To Err Is Human"[1] concluded that 44,000 to 98,000 people a year die from medical errors, at a cost of $17–29 billion per year. A more recent study puts the estimate at 100,000–400,000 deaths per year.[2] Here's a quote from the latter:

> In a sense, it does not matter whether the deaths of 100,000, 200,000 or 400,000 Americans each year are associated with PAE (Preventable Adverse Effects) in hospitals. Any of these estimates demand assertive action.

Jenny's story is, unfortunately, not uncommon. These situations happen every day, and not only in the US. However, it's important not to blame the nurses, or we miss the entire context that led up to these grave mistakes. There's a concept used in the healthcare field called the *Swiss Cheese model* of accident causation. This model (see Figure 1-2) compares human systems to multiple slices of holed cheese.

There may be multiple layers to pass through before a mistake affects the patient. For example, when there is a medication error, the source of the error can occur in any of these "layers": the doctor's prescription, the pharmacist filling it, the medication being stocked correctly, the nurse preparing and giving it, and the mechanism used to administer it to the patient. Each layer has its own holes (flaws in the preventative measures), but together they reduce the chances of an error happening. In our example, nurses were the last layer of defense, so it's easy to blame them for the mistake that happened. But in fact, interface design should act as the last layer in that model. It usually accomplishes that by reducing the cognitive load required to complete a task, thus allowing more resources to be dedicated to error prevention. Unfortunately, in the healthcare industry, it instead leads to making more holes.

1   Kohn, Linda T., Janet M. Corrigan, and Molla S. Donaldson, eds. "To Err Is Human: Building a Safer Health System." Washington, DC: The National Academies Press, 2000.
2   James, J. T. "A New, Evidence-Based Estimate of Patient Harms Associated with Hospital Care." *Journal of Patient Safety* 9:3 (2013): 122–128. doi:10.1097/pts.0b013e3182948a69

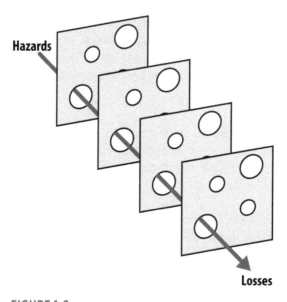

Hazards

Losses

FIGURE 1-2.
The Swiss Cheese model of how errors can make it through many layers of imperfect prevention methods

Cognitive capacity is the total amount of information the brain is capable of retaining at any moment. This amount is limited and can't be stretched. In the case of Jenny, the software was most likely overloading the nurses' cognitive capacity by forcing them to figure out how to use the interface to chart the patient's care and make the appropriate orders. Nurses (and all medical staff, really) are working in an environment and with tools that are working against them. With thousands of medical errors happening every year, it is apparent that there is more to this problem than negligence. The system is broken, and design should be doing its part in repairing it.

It is important to note that a better user interface alone is not the solution. Since it's our area of concern, however, we should study its role and improve that layer as best we can. Technology and design in healthcare should be used as a protective layer, to ensure mistakes don't happen. In the case of Jenny, technology was instead a key factor in a tragic error.

The Role and Responsibilities of Designers

If you ask 10 designers what their role is, chances are you will get 10 completely different answers.

Design, as Jared Spool so succinctly put it, is "the rendering of intent."[3] While that is a very correct, logical, and concise way of boiling it down, for user experience designers it misses one important element: people. We would define design, especially in the sense of designing products and software people will use, as "the planning of a product's interaction with people."

Good designs are the ones that are transparent, delightful, and/or helpful. Therefore, bad designs are the ones that collide with human behaviors and cause undesired friction. When we create things without the end users in mind (or with some vague sense of them as customers), we almost always end up creating bad designs. *Badly designed products serve their creator (or sponsor) first and the users second.* Good design attempts to understand the intended users and create an experience that serves their needs. A good design is a worthwhile one; one whose existence isn't a burden on its users, but instead makes their lives better in some way. Fortunately, good design isn't just a bunch of goodwill and pleasant feelings—it's good business too. Spending resources on design is a worthwhile investment. Some professionals go as far as saying that every dollar spent on user experience brings up to $100 in return.[4] If one product serves its creator first and its competitor serves the customers, then it's most likely that the customers will choose the latter. In today's technology landscape, it's easier than ever for competitors to match features and scale up to millions of users. Thus, user-centered design, because of its accessible nature, becomes the main differentiator.

THE CLIENT PARADOX

Designers often, and rightfully, claim credit for the success of a product. Wouldn't it be fair to blame them for unsuccessful products too?

---

3 Spool, Jared M. "Design Is the Rendering of Intent." UIE, December 30, 2013, *https://articles.uie.com/design_rendering_intent.*

4 Spillers, Frank. "Making a Strong Business Case for the ROI of UX [Infographic]." Experience Dynamics, July 24, 2014, *http://bit.ly/1t6a1rk.*

There are many blogs that specialize in cataloging examples of bad design. When we witness such examples, it seems natural to blame the designers (and laugh, let's be honest) for their poor work, lack of empathy, or basic skills. However, this doesn't paint the complete picture. The reality is often that the designer answers to a client. Tim Parsons, in his book *Thinking Objects: Contemporary Approaches to Product Design* (AVA Publishing), criticizes this aspect of the design practice. The paradox comes from the fact that designers aren't always in charge, since they get paid by a client that has a vision, business needs, objectives, etc., and not by the users that will end up using the design. This places the designers in a rather awkward position. We have heard countless times, "I ended up doing what the client wanted." Unfortunately, there is no magical solution to this issue.

When commissioned with a project that "feels wrong" to them, designers should do everything in their power to educate their client. It might take more time, but the responsibility falls on them. If they have the means, they can simply refuse to do the work, but that is quite idealistic, and we understand that only privileged designers and design firms can take such a drastic stand. Moreover, if one refuses to do the work, a less scrupulous designer may end up doing it, and probably cause even more damage.

We know that, at some point in our careers, we all have to make tough calls. Sometimes we have to choose our client's needs over the users' needs. When this is acceptable and when it is not is a difficult line to draw. Many occupations have established codes of ethics that are taught in school and enforced by their professional orders. These guiding principles help in making fair decisions in complex situations, while protecting the clients, the users, and the professionals doing the work. Several codes for graphic design exist, but none are widely distributed or enforced. While the International Council of Design's model of a code of conduct (*http://www.ico-d.org/database/files/library/icoD_BP_CodeofConduct.pdf*) is a good start, we feel it's incomplete and won't help in making a fair decision in many of the situations cited in this book. The best code of conduct, in our humble opinion, was written by a group of students and professors and is called "Ethics for the Starving Designer" (*http://www.starvingforethics.com*). The first principle is a great starting point:

Finding the most ethical course of action will sometimes be difficult, but that difficulty will not deter me from striving to find the most ethical solution to any problem I may encounter. If I find myself in a situation where I have made a decision that I am unhappy with, I will instead endeavour to make an ethical decision for myself and for others in the future. While some circumstances may force me to compromise at times, I will not resign to turning to compromise in future situations, and will face my next ethical decision with a renewed determination to find the best outcome.

Every designer should write down what they stand for, what they think is acceptable or not. Having this "will never do" list will help you make difficult decisions when they arise.

UNDERSTANDING AND IDENTIFYING HIDDEN COSTS

Often, those of us who are passionate about technology get caught up in the science and exploration of it. We gawk over all the possibilities it enables, and rarely stop to think about the "why" of it. We are responsible for what we bring into this world, in the same way that parents are responsible for their children. Yet we often create at a whim, chasing the next idea, the next dollar, the next trend. Asking if what we are building should even exist is important not only from a philosophical or moral standpoint, but also from a business perspective. Furthermore, we must ask ourselves: is our success coming at a hidden cost? For some companies that might be at the cost of the environment; for others, it can be at the cost of their own employees' well-being or their customers' trust. We are often fooled into thinking that what we made was successful, when in reality the cost is hidden or externalized. Failing to identify all of the hidden costs and the impact of our designs on the world around us can lead us to blindly and unintentionally cause harm to others.

In order to identify and avoid these potential hidden costs, we suggest creating lists of "goals," "non-goals," and "anti-goals" (also called "hazards"). They can be added to the product brief or creative brief, if your company uses these. While the concept of "goals" is pretty straightforward, the two latter sections are rarely found in product design briefs. The list of "non-goals" aims at setting objectives that are explicitly out of scope for the current effort. While this might sound unnecessary, in our experience there is value to being explicit about things that are out of scope, in case there is ambiguity about the boundaries around one or more goals, or any tendency toward "scope creep." The third section, "anti-goals," is used to describe things you really, really don't want to happen. This section should be followed by descriptions of how you will make sure the anti-goals don't happen, with precise test objectives. We call these "safeguards."

For example, here's what a brief for a new subscription page on a website might look like with the three types of goals outlined:

- Goals (this feature will):
    - Allow customers to sign up to the service.
    - Make the subscription flow seamless to make sure we don't lose conversions in the process.
    - Highlight all the benefits of our service by comparing them to our competitor.
- Non-goals (this feature shouldn't):
    - Impact the content on the home page.
    - Change the login and password validation.
    - Impact the first page seen once logged in.
- Anti-goals (this feature will not):
    - Confuse the potential customers with a hidden pricing structure.
    - Hide the fact that the service charges automatically unless they unsubscribe from it.
    - Make the cancellation flow more complex.
    - Have an impact on the amount of customer service tickets.
- Safeguards:
    - We will test that the potential customers understand the pricing structure and the subscription model before they sign up. We will do this through user testing.
    - We will monitor customer service calls and will offer modifications to the page, should we notice confusion.

Conclusion

Without good design, technology quickly turns from a help to a harm. It can kill, but that isn't the only negative effect. It can cause *emotional harm*, like when a social app facilitates bullying. It can cause *exclusion*, like when a seeing-impaired person doesn't get to participate in socializing on a popular website because simple accessibility best practices have not been attended to. It can cause *injustice*, like nullifying someone's vote, or simply cause *frustration* by neglecting a user's preferences.

Designers are gatekeepers of technology. They have a critical role to play in the way technology will impact people's lives. It is up to us to ensure the gates are as wide open and accessible as possible.

In the following chapters, you will read testimonials from people generously recounting how technology impacted them negatively. We also have interviews with great designers who all try, in their own way, to benefit society through their work. We will dig deep into stories of how bad design interferes with people's lives in very real ways. We will explore extreme examples, as well as more common ones that designers may face in their careers. While we do our best to add practical pieces of advice about how we can tackle these difficult issues, we don't claim to have all the answers. Our main goal is to shed light on these areas, to call attention to how bad design affects people's lives. That's the most important step to solving any big problem: highlighting it.

Key Takeaways

1. Blaming the last people involved in a process for making a costly mistake is not productive. They are generally just one of the multiple layers of the Swiss Cheese model.

2. Good visual design reduces the cognitive load required to complete a task.

3. Badly designed products serve their creator (or sponsor) first and the user second.

4. Designers are not always in charge, since they often answer to a client. When confronted with design solutions they are not comfortable with, designers have the responsibility to educate their clients.

5. Hidden costs often fool us into thinking that what we made was successful, when in reality the cost is hidden or externalized. Failing to identify all of the hidden costs and the impact of our designs on the world around us can lead to blindly and unintentionally causing harm to others.

6. Designers are gatekeepers of technology. They have a critical role to play in the way technology will impact people's lives. It is up to us to ensure the gates are as wide open and accessible as possible.

Interview with Amy Cueva

The following is an interview with Amy Cueva, Founder and Chief Experience Officer at Mad*Pow. Mad*Pow is an award-winning agency that works with a wide variety of companies ranging from Fortune 500s to startups. It organizes a yearly conference for healthcare design called HXD and is located in Portsmouth, NH.

1. How do you see bad design affecting healthcare?

There is plenty of bad design in healthcare. As an industry, it lags in its acceptance of and investment in design. Design problems manifest through visual design, interface design, information design, and usability. But the biggest issues are systemic and experiential in nature. Examples of those issues include:

Electronic medical records (EMRs)
> The need to interact with an EMR takes a lot of time and also creates a physical boundary and distraction between the patient and the doctor, removing the humanity from the interaction and making it more transactional in nature. EMRs are essentially the interface to a database of medical information on a patient.

Health insurance plan selection (US)
> People have a hard time figuring out which plan is right for them because they are comparing plans based upon terms they don't understand or that are difficult to put into context. It is hard to discern what your overall cost and quality of care will be with one plan vs. another plan.

Silos and aversion to risk

Health organizations are siloed inside themselves and among themselves. This inhibits the collaboration that would lead to better designs-for an improved health experience. Health organizations have been built to avoid risk, but in order to innovate a small amount of risk is necessary to explore new concepts and test them. This involves a culture shift that is difficult, and takes time.

Decision support and interventions

We have reams of data around the treatments that are most efficacious and the care pathways that will work best. We talk about big data, but we struggle to get the right information to the right person at the right time. This is a design problem, but also a technology and organizational problem.

Prevention is difficult to monetize

[The US] healthcare system is mostly sickcare. The system is designed to care for people once something happens to them, not work with them to prevent something from happening. Prevention is an investment, and one many organizations are not willing to make because there is no immediate profit to be had or it is deemed to be someone else's problem. Now that the healthcare system is getting to the crisis point it is becoming a problem for all of us.

2. How do you think design will be able to change healthcare?

I believe that human-centered design will inspire our direction, fuel business innovation, and deliver positive human impact, helping us to improve the experience of health. I believe design and designers play an essential role in improving the experience of health. As designers we advocate for the people who will be affected by our designs, we are engaged by our empathy, we envision a better future, we paint the picture for everyone to see, and then we bring people along with us to make that future a reality.

We need to make the customer, the patient, the person the focus of our efforts, because right now they are left to navigate a very disconnected ecosystem on their own. The health system functions but does not get as close to whole health as we would hope possible considering our human capacity to care, connect, and innovate. But we can move beyond the transactional. We can build trust with those we serve. We can be there when they need us most. We can begin to become their partner throughout their health journey, tracing their path through the ecosystem, identifying unmet needs and organizations that have shared objectives. We know that silos exist both inside and outside of our health organizations, but I believe that new forms of collaboration will help us to break down walls and will lead to unprecedented innovation and unimaginable results.

New partnerships and shared services will help us start to break down walls and address the pain points and unmet needs present in the current health ecosystem.

3. How can designers help?

Designers can help by understanding the needs of the people they are designing for as fully as possible and advocating for those people. Designers can connect the experience that will be of most benefit to the people the organization serves back to the organization's purpose, making the business case for investing in it. Designers can make the risks associated with bad design and the benefits associated with good design clear. Designers can practice human-centered design methods and invite others to the table to participate so that their eyes can be opened to the efficacy of the approach.

Designers can follow, contribute to, and relate aspects of the Designers Oath (*http://www.designersoath.com*) to the focus of their organization. Designers can scan the ecosystem for organizations that have shared objectives and explore how those organizations or other existing information, resources, or services could be integrated into the solution.

Designers are engaged by their empathy, envision a better future, and paint the picture for others to see. Designers serve an essential role of imagining and illustrating that there is a better way and can get people excited to blaze that new trail together.

4. How can the layperson help?

The layperson can make it their business to know what an organization stands for—what is its purpose beyond profit, and how that organization brings that purpose to life in all that it does. Then they can make decisions around who to do business with based upon how the organization's purpose aligns with what they are passionate about as individuals. A layperson can ask an organization how it involves patients, customers, people in the creation and improvement of its processes, policies, and systems.

5. What role does design have in making the world a better place to live?

Customer focus and empathy-inspired design is not idealism, it is good business—and a practice that can also deliver positive impact at the societal level. In her [2015] *Harvard Business Review* article "Corporate Empathy Is Not an Oxymoron," Belinda Parmar says, "There is nothing soft about it. Empathy is a hard skill that should be required from the board-room to the shop floor." And this empathy will inspire how we design our products, services, partnerships, and organizations. It is an experience economy. Organizations in other industries have realized this. In financial services, for example, it is not about just selling products and services or enabling customers to complete self-service transactions easily; it is about the relationship the people have with the organization and the perceived benefits of that relationship. Imagine the potential here, if a large national bank helped its customers save 5% more. That would be of benefit to that bank, and of course to those individuals, but it would also have tremendous impact on society as a whole.

As organizations operationalize their purpose, we will see the Corporate Social Responsibility and Customer Experience disciplines converge. And it goes beyond the marketing message or the advertising campaign; purpose-driven companies will build momentum and traction around their purpose by weaving it into all business functions and gain competitive advantage as a result. It isn't enough to make a profit anymore. This calls us to move beyond the standard boundaries that have defined our organizations in the past.

We see these boundaries begin to shift as insurers aim to help their members get healthier and not just be their "adjudication partner" and as pharma companies explore digital "therapies" in addition to drugs.

Profit can be delivered with consideration for customer needs and motivations *and* without taking advantage of them. A decided understanding of how the decisions an organization makes will impact society, unintended consequences, and associated ethics will be required.

Consumers are more and more aware of the impact corporations make on society every day and it is informing the decisions they make around who to do business with. Impact-focused organizations will align with the passions of their customer base and will thereby be differentiated in the marketplace. This stance requires taking the long view, an understanding of long-term impact and not just short-term returns.

6. What can designers add to their process in order to avoid causing harm in this way?

We can become students of the problem, inclusive in our approach. In getting outside the four walls of our typical environment and getting face time with the people we serve we can come to a deeper understanding of what will drive real meaning and value in the context of their lives—what will truly motivate, engage, inform, guide, and comfort. Humans are complicated. The richness of detail in the story provides us with both information and inspiration.

Clayton Christensen discusses the importance of theories in guiding disruptive innovation and points out that "it is by understanding the people we serve in the present that we construct a theory about the future." Ethnographic research, where we talk with and observe real people in their "native habitat," helps us to develop a rich understanding of current problems and unmet needs such that we can create solid theories that will guide our efforts moving forward. In addition, it activates our empathy and provides needed inspiration for our creativity. For example, if we want folks managing chronic conditions to not use the ER as their primary care office, have we been in the ER and spoken with people there or are we making assumptions around why they are there and how the situation might be improved?

Integrate empathy-building activities into the process and start to focus on empathy as an organization. We can encourage stakeholders at our organizations to get involved in ethnographic studies, participatory and collaborative design methods, and validation activities like usability, usefulness, desirability, and efficacy testing. Companies that do this on an ongoing basis will receive the rich information that will guide experiential improvements for years to come.

Through research we come to understand emotion. Emotion will show us where we need to focus, where we are doing well, and where we need to improve. The emotions of the people we serve matter. They affect the trajectory of their path forward. Not just the emotion of the people we serve, but our emotion as well. We need to allow ourselves to feel. Emotion moves us beyond cognitive knowing to visceral knowing—that gut feeling we get inspires our curiosity, powers our imagination, enhances our wisdom, leads us to take action, and motivates us to persevere.

We can consider the full range of emotions and situations people will bring to their experiences via personas. In walking in the shoes of the people we serve we can explore how to make things better for them. Personas can contain not just demographic information, but also behavioral, psychographic, and emotional information. Personas can guide our teams in making decisions about the experience, but personas alone are not enough.

We can formulate a "hierarchy of needs" based on research insights to focus our experiential efforts and measure our performance. For example: *Trustworthy*—I got the information and utility I needed at every touchpoint I needed it; *Easy*—This company, product, or service is easy to do business with; *Kind*—I felt like they were considering my needs and that I was treated well; *Meaningful*—It was meaningful to my life, I achieved a greater outcome or received an unanticipated benefit; *Very Cool*—Wow, that was actually very cool.

Many in our industry suffer from "shiny object syndrome," where we oftentimes want to jump to very cool without having delivered trust, ease, kindness, and meaning. We can audit the ecosystem of interaction, examining each touchpoint from the perspective of each persona and their hierarchy of needs, starting at the bottom and working toward the top.

We can scan the marketplace to understand what other solutions and entities are in the picture and figure out how to integrate with them or cooperate with them and be aware of them so that we can start to connect elements of the experience together on behalf of the patient. We can audit present experiences and future state theories against the organization's purpose beyond profit as well.

The experience is a byproduct of how we are organized internally to deliver it. If we are a mess on the inside, the resulting experience will be a mess as well. It isn't enough to imagine an amazing experience. We also need to bring that experience to market. In order to deliver exceptional experiences, we will need to help our organizations transform themselves into being empathy driven and customer focused in all they do. We will continue to investigate models for communicating the benefits of empathy-inspired design to executives and decision makers, immersing them in the process, and providing them with essential training, methods, and tools to aid their efforts. And training does help! Telefonica Germany was able to see a 6% improvement in customer satisfaction within six months of implementing an enterprise-level empathy training program.

In the *HBR* article I mentioned earlier, "Corporate Empathy Is Not an Oxymoron," Belinda points out that empathy can be measured, but also that "Serious people will regularly dismiss empathy for the more concrete and defensible virtues of rational analysis." I would argue that rational analysis does not supply the richness of inspiration that empathy and human-centered design do—inspiration that will fuel both experiential and disruptive innovation. But don't stop with measuring your organization's empathy. Consider how to measure performance on the customer hierarchy of needs and the organization's purpose. Create incentive programs and bonus structures that stem from these measures. Many companies have found that when incentive programs aligned with customer-focused measurements, rapid improvements were achieved in short order. One company that we work with has assembled an interdisciplinary team that evaluates whether business decisions will have a positive, negative, or neutral impact on the customer experience. If the anticipated impact is negative, there is an escalation path available to remedy the situation. Decision-making frameworks can help, but avoid creating a culture where numbers strip the humanity out of the decision-making process.

[2]

Design Can Kill

When designing for digital mediums, it's easy to become detached from how design decisions affect the end user. The word "user" itself can be a vehicle for that detachment. When the "user" doesn't have a face and a name, it becomes a formless concept, blending in with other quantitative metrics and taking on any assumed needs to justify business decisions. It quickly becomes a number on a crowded dashboard, and its reaction to the product is just another metric to consider in an effort to increase revenue.

Increasing a company's revenue isn't an issue per se, the same way that tracking success metrics isn't necessarily problematic. But because of their dry nature, quantitative metrics often lie on the opposite end of the spectrum from empathy. They can contribute to objectifying and depersonalizing users. They also conveniently prevent us from feeling the discomfort of empathy, the shame and guilt if users get hurt. Historically, metrics have been underused by UX designers. We think that owning them might help in ensuring they aren't used as a way to objectify and depersonalize the users. Therefore, it is important to find a balance between qualitative and quantitative metrics. Research shows that it's easy to feel strong emotions for a close group of people, but it's harder to scale that care out to thousands of users whom we have never met.[1] This isn't an excuse to shed responsibility, though. The potential effects of our work should constantly be on our mind. That's why user interviews and observations are so helpful—yet a surprising number of designers have never seen their products being used by a real user.

---

1   Brashears, Matthew E. "Humans Use Compression Heuristics to Improve the Recall of Social Networks." *Scientific Reports* 3 (2013): 1513–0151. doi:10.1038/srep01513

Stupid Errors Versus Stupid Users

It is easy to blame disasters and errors on the inability of the user. There are actually a variety of slang words used within the tech circle, all with derogatory meanings, to indicate that the user is the problem. That the user is stupid. Have you ever heard of the acronym PEBKAC? It stands for "Problem Exists Between Keyboard and Chair." Or a "type 16" error? Meaning that the error is not in the computer but 16 inches away from the screen (the user, again). Even in the US Navy and Army, there are slang terms to mock user errors. The Navy uses "Eye-Dee-Ten-Tango" (ID10T).[2] In the Army it's "One-Delta-Ten-Tango" (1D10T). Although this might sound funny and like just another office joke, thinking that way creates a distance between the "intelligent" creator and the "stupid" user. This indifference can lead to irresponsibility, prejudice, intolerance, and contempt. It also prevents us from learning important lessons that can be gleaned from errors and tragedies.

After all, maybe most bugs are type 16: 16 inches from the *designer's* screen.

A good designer should constantly be looking for opportunities to learn from others' mistakes. Instead of blaming the protagonists, we should try to put ourselves in their shoes and honestly answer these questions: What would lead me to design the same interface they did? What decisions led to this product being approved and shipped? How can I avoid finding myself in a similar position in the future?

When studying an incident in retrospect, we want to know if it could have been prevented. This is where a Use Error Chart is extremely useful (see Figure 2-1). We encourage you to refer to this chart when critiquing any design. If the error was caused by an action that lives in the "normal use" spectrum, then it should have been planned and accounted for by the conception team. If the error was caused by an intended action that lives outside of normal use, then it would be very critical to blame solely the designers. However, if the consequence of an error outside of normal use is potentially very severe, then the team should attempt to mitigate it. We will address these situations in Chapter 4, and suggest techniques to come up with as many potential harmful use cases as possible.

---

2 "NAVspeak Glossary," Usna.org. Archived from the original on 1 December 2010.

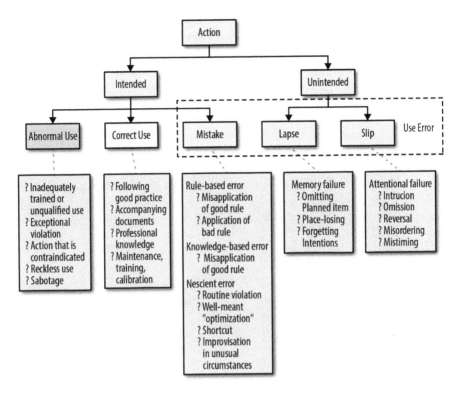

FIGURE 2-1.
Use Error Chart inspired by IEC 62366:2007. This chart can be referred to when studying an incident in hindsight. It helps in answering the question, "Could this incident have been be prevented?"

In this chapter, we will share a broad range of case studies where bad design caused physical harm. We don't want to fall into sensationalism with the following examples, nor do we assume that bad design was always the sole cause of the disasters. Sometimes the designs were really good, but failed at planning for certain use cases that led to these incidents. We want to treat these examples as learning opportunities, so we'll focus on the role played by design in causing physical harm and what should be done to avoid similar situations in the future.

Case Study 1: Therac-25

The Therac-25 (see Figure 2-2) was a radiotherapy machine designed to deliver radiation in a safe dosage using either an electron or x-ray beam. It was preceded by two earlier versions, the Therac-6 and Therac-20. Radiation therapy is generally part of a cancer treatment to control or kill malignant cells. The story of the Therac-25 is a textbook example, used by many computer science classes. It illustrates perfectly how software can harm people. Between 1985 and 1987, six accidents involving massive overdoses to patients occurred. Three of the patients involved in these incidents later died from their injuries, and the others were seriously harmed. Thankfully, only 11 machines were ever installed and they were later recalled for extensive design changes, including hardware safeguards against software errors.

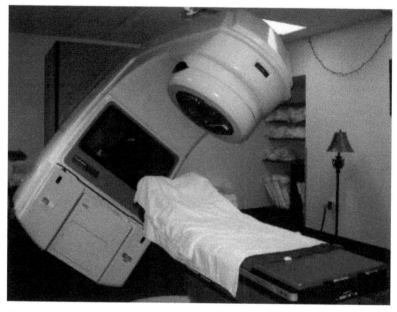

FIGURE 2-2.
The Therac-25 radiation therapy machine (source: *http://www.idg.bg*)

The operator of the Therac-25 would input the prescribed dose and mode to be administered by the machine. The problem was that in rare instances the machine would blast the patient with thousands of rad (radiation absorbed dose). In some cases, the dose went up to 17,000 rad (the typical single therapeutic dose is 200 rad.) The immediate pain of receiving such a high dose was so intense that, in one case, the patient leaped from the operating table and ran out of the room. The effect on the body in the following weeks was even more frightening—considering that a blast of 1,000 rad over the whole body is considered to be fatal, it's easy to imagine the disastrous effect of 17,000 rad blasted into a dime-sized area. The first day following the faulty treatment, the patient experienced rashes and burn marks. Then, over the next few weeks, the wound developed into a large hole, resembling "a slow motion gunshot."[3] When patients reported their injuries the company behind the device first denied it was a problem, and stated that it was impossible. The bugs in the Therac-25 and the issues that caused it are now well documented.

INTERFACE DIAGNOSIS

In order to formulate an unbiased critique of the interface, we will use the 10 Usability Heuristics for Interface Design, created by Jakob Nielsen (*https://www.nngroup.com/articles/ten-usability-heuristics*). We could have used other lists, such as Theo Mandel's list of Golden Rules (*http://bit.ly/2o2Q8cr*) or Bruce Tognazzini's First Principles of Interaction Design (*http://bit.ly/2oCcoro*). These are all great resources that are well worth the reading effort. However, we decided to use Nielsen's for its simplicity and ease of understanding. Even though this list was created over 20 years ago, these heuristics are still being used broadly in the industry and are considered best practices. We are not blaming the company behind the Therac-25 for not using these heuristics, because they simply didn't exist back then. The industry was still figuring out the best practices for interface design.

As a reminder, here's the list taken from Nielsen Norman Group's website:

1. Visibility of system status

   The system should always keep users informed about what is going on, through appropriate feedback within reasonable time.

2. Match between system and the real world

   The system should speak the users' language, with words, phrases and concepts familiar to the user, rather than system-oriented terms. Follow real-world conventions, making information appear in a natural and logical order.

3. User control and freedom

---

3   Rose, Barbara Wade. "Fatal Dose: Radiation Deaths Linked to AECL Computer Errors." CCNR, June 1994, *http://www.ccnr.org/fatal_dose.html*.

Users often choose system functions by mistake and will need a clearly marked "emergency exit" to leave the unwanted state without having to go through an extended dialogue. Support undo and redo.

4. Consistency and standards

Users should not have to wonder whether different words, situations, or actions mean the same thing. Follow platform conventions.

5. Error prevention

Even better than good error messages is a careful design which prevents a problem from occurring in the first place. Either eliminate error-prone conditions or check for them and present users with a confirmation option before they commit to the action.

6. Recognition rather than recall

Minimize the user's memory load by making objects, actions, and options visible. The user should not have to remember information from one part of the dialogue to another. Instructions for use of the system should be visible or easily retrievable whenever appropriate.

7. Flexibility and efficiency of use

Accelerators—unseen by the novice user—may often speed up the interaction for the expert user such that the system can cater to both inexperienced and experienced users. Allow users to tailor frequent actions.

8. Aesthetic and minimalist design

Dialogues should not contain information which is irrelevant or rarely needed. Every extra unit of information in a dialogue competes with the relevant units of information and diminishes their relative visibility.

9. Help users recognize, diagnose, and recover from errors

Error messages should be expressed in plain language (no codes), precisely indicate the problem, and constructively suggest a solution.

10. Help and documentation

Even though it is better if the system can be used without documentation, it may be necessary to provide help and documentation. Any such information should be easy to search, focused on the user's task, list concrete steps to be carried out, and not be too large.

First issue

Let's take a look at the user interface issues of the Therac-25. Although the interface is not the only factor that led to the mistakes that were made, we believe that it played a significant part. For example, in one of the fatal instances, the operator was inputting the prescribed dose while the patient lay in the radiation room. The Therac-25 interface required the operator to input the prescribed dose of radiation after choosing a mode (see Figure 2-3). According to a lecture by UC Berkeley Computer Science professor Brian Harvey, the operator typed in the required mode (the choices being "e" for electron or "x" for x-ray) and moved to the next field. The operator then realized they had input the incorrect mode and attempted to navigate back up to that field by pressing the up arrow a few times (remember that we are in the '80s; they were not using a mouse).

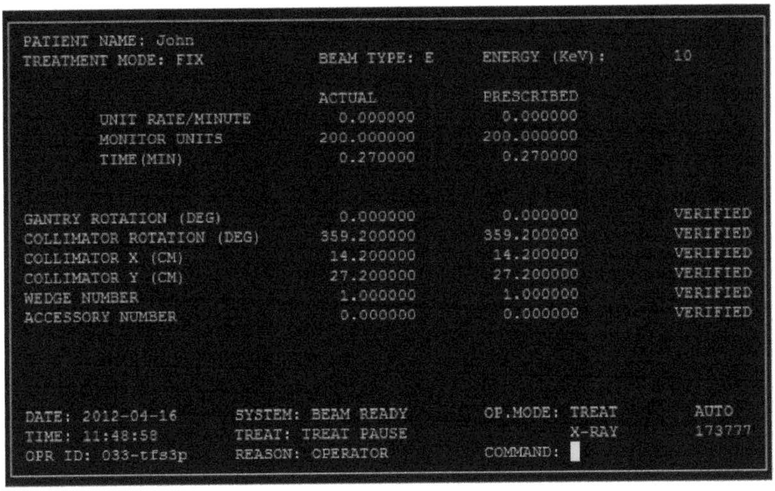

```
PATIENT NAME: John
TREATMENT MODE: FIX          BEAM TYPE: E      ENERGY (KeV):        10

                             ACTUAL            PRESCRIBED
          UNIT RATE/MINUTE    0.000000          0.000000
          MONITOR UNITS     200.000000        200.000000
          TIME(MIN)           0.270000          0.270000


GANTRY ROTATION (DEG)         0.000000          0.000000        VERIFIED
COLLIMATOR ROTATION (DEG)   359.200000        359.200000        VERIFIED
COLLIMATOR X (CM)            14.200000         14.200000        VERIFIED
COLLIMATOR Y (CM)            27.200000         27.200000        VERIFIED
WEDGE NUMBER                  1.000000          1.000000        VERIFIED
ACCESSORY NUMBER              0.000000          0.000000        VERIFIED



DATE: 2012-04-16    SYSTEM: BEAM READY      OP.MODE: TREAT        AUTO
TIME: 11:48:58      TREAT: TREAT PAUSE              X-RAY       173777
OPR ID: 033-tfs3p   REASON: OPERATOR        COMMAND: █
```

FIGURE 2-3.
A command-line interface, similar to what the Therac-25's interface would have looked like (source: Wikibooks)

When trying to correct the mistake, the operator didn't notice that pressing the up arrow key did not move the cursor. Instead, it input the string of characters that represents the up arrow key. This string of characters was the programmatic signal a keyboard gave a computer program to identify what key was pressed.

This clearly breaks the first rule on Jakob Nielsen's list: "Visibility of system status." Not only would an operator never want to input the up arrow key string of characters into any text field, but the interface should always communicate what is going on. Users should not have to wonder what is entered, nor should they have to review whether what they have entered made it to the end correctly. It might sound pretty obvious, but the software should *always* display what the user is actually typing.

Second issue

The next interface issue is that when nothing was added to one of these fields, it would assume a default value. This also breaks Nielsen's first rule. Defaults can sometimes be very useful in preventing errors, but they are definitely not desired when designing a machine that administers radiation dosages specific to patients, prescribed by their doctor. This is even more dangerous when the default values are not shown. If the default values are hidden from the user, it might lead to unintentional actions and confusion.

Third issue

The third interface issue concerns the error messages. In another instance, after the operator had finished and executed the form, the Therac-25 software returned an error. Error handling is a very good practice. Unfortunately, in this case, it simply read "Malfunction 54," which isn't descriptive enough to actually understand what the mistake is and how to fix it. When using the Therac-25, similarly vague error messages occurred frequently. This operator had become accustomed to pressing the "p" key to override error messages everywhere in the process. Being so used to seeing illegitimate errors, the operator simply ignored the one that caused the overdose in this deadly instance. After bypassing the error message the first time (and unknowingly blasting the patient), the operator saw it again. Every time the error was overruled, in the other room, the patient was zapped with 15,000–16,000 rad. The patient had previously been treated by the machine and knew that this pain was unusual, and attempted to call for help. He struggled to the floor, made his way to the door and banged on it to get someone's attention. Usually, the operator would see and hear the patient via a camera and intercom system placed in the treatment room. Unfortunately, both were out of order that day. The patient returned to the hospital a few weeks later spitting blood: the doctors diagnosed radiation overexposure. The experience paralyzed his left arm, legs, left vocal cord, and diaphragm. He died five months later.

Error messages should follow Nielsen's Usability Heuristics 5, 7, and 9. The best error message is no error message at all! The Therac-25's software should have been easy to use, presented predictable actions, and offered live validation. An interface should know the purpose of its design, and action outside of a reasonable range should set the interface to guide the user back to the proper interactions.

A great example of error prevention from live validation is seen in sign-up forms, where the new user has to select a username (see Figure 2-4). When typing, users instantly see if their desired name is available or not, preventing them from having to validate the form before learning that they have to come up with a new one. We also frequently see live error validation in forms asking the user to confirm their password by retyping it. If they don't match, the field automatically turns red, indicating that there's a mismatch that prevents the user from continuing to the next step.

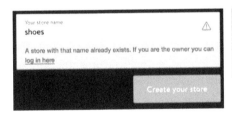

FIGURE 2-4.
A live validation example from shopify.com. If the store name entered is not available, the user is presented with the option to log in.

In the case of the Therac-25, the amount of illegitimate errors the operator had been accustomed to seeing made them blind to the messages on the screen. Think of how easily one can ignore a banner ad, or a modal window asking to perform an update...for the 12th time in the same week. Even when they use intense language, warnings, or flashing colors, we are trained to ignore them. Just like in the fable of "The Boy Who Cried Wolf," many important warning messages are missed because they have proven useless in the past. This concept is usually referred to as *banner blindness*, and it also applies to confirmation messages. A good practice is to avoid constantly asking confirmation for user-generated actions if they are not destructive, or if they can be reverted. Because of the overwhelming number of confirmation modals we're exposed to, users tend to grow accustomed to clicking "confirm" without even reading the warning or the instruction.

A good example of an interface not asking for useless confirmation is the email service Gmail. When an email is deleted, instead of asking the user "Are you sure you want to delete this email?" it will automatically perform the requested action, and let you "undo" if you have indeed made a mistake (see Figure 2-5). This is less obtrusive but still provides a way to recover in instances where you delete an email unintentionally and need to get it back.

FIGURE 2-5.
Gmail's Inbox undo. Note the yellow banner offering the user the choice to undo the action, instead of prompting with a confirmation modal.

Lastly, in the case of the Therac-25 software the design of the error messages should have been a lot more informative and useful. The message "Malfunction 54" conveys nothing to the operator about the issue. Is there a mistake in the form? Is the machine broken? Do they need to call a technician or should they simply try again? Even worse, "Malfunction 54" was not listed in the user manual of the machine. Operators couldn't even look it up if they wanted to. The error message should have told the operator exactly what was going wrong and provided an action to fix it: for example, warning that the value for the radiation was above an acceptable range, then leading the user back to the form with the faulty field highlighted.

TESTING IS NOT OPTIONAL

If the creators of the Therac-25 had made design (specifically usability) a requirement on its launch list, these deaths and injuries would have been prevented. In a product development cycle, when the deadlines and budgets are tight, the quality of error messages can seem trivial. Spending a lot of time and effort on a small part of the product (the interface only a group of trained technicians will use) can easily get deprioritized. To combat this, in response to incidents like those associated with the Therac-25, the International Electrotechnical Commission has created a life cycle development standard (*https://webstore.iec.ch/publication/22794*) for medical device software.

To learn from these kinds of accidents and to prevent them in the future, we must not simply blame the company and engineers that worked on the development of these products. Most accidents involving complex technologies are caused by a combination of many factors (organizational, managerial, technical, and even political). All software, even if extremely well designed, will behave in an unexpected way under certain conditions. As designers, it's hard to plan for every potential error and bug. This is why we can't stress enough the importance of resolving issues that are easily identifiable. These systems can't fail basic usability guidelines; there is too much at stake for design to be an afterthought. It's also important to note that very simple user testing would have helped identify most of these common errors. *When it comes to medical interfaces, testing with real users in realistic scenarios is not optional.*

Case Study 2: Ferry Crash in New York City

On the morning of January 9, 2013, 300 passengers slowly boarded the ferry that crosses the river from Seastreak to Wall Street. It was just another day commuting into New York City. But as the ferry neared the pier to dock, something went wrong: instead of slowing down, the ferry accelerated. It rushed toward the pier at 12 knots (about 14 miles per hour) and struck a second pier, causing a sudden jolt that sent passengers and glass debris flying. When the ferry finally came to a stop, 79 people had been injured. It was reported that 75 sustained minor injuries and 4 were seriously injured.

It is important that we define what "minor" and "serious" injuries are. Glossing over statistics is easy, especially ones with terms that can be misleading or ambiguous. We should be very wary of euphemisms used when stories are being reported, especially by company spokespeople. A "minor" injury is not necessarily as minor as one might imagine, as this definition makes plain:

> A minor injury means a sprain, strain, whiplash associated disorder, contusion, abrasion, laceration or subluxation and any clinically associated sequelae. This term is to be interpreted to apply where a person sustains any one or more of these injuries.[4]

According to this definition, someone with multiple fractures would be considered a victim with "minor" injuries. If you have suffered an open fracture or seen someone with one, you will understand that it doesn't feel "minor" at all! Article 51 of the New York Insurance Law (*http://www.dfs.ny.gov/insurance/r68/r68_art51.htm*) defines a "serious" injury as follows:

> A physical injury which creates a substantial risk of death, or which causes serious disfigurement, serious impairment of health or serious loss or impairment of the function of any bodily organ.

In the aftermath of the ferry crash, many were laid on stretchers with neck braces. One victim reported that he could not move for 10 to 15 minutes because of the immense pain in his arms and legs. In her opening statement on the disaster (*https://app.ntsb.gov/news/speeches/hersman/daph140408.html*), Deborah A. P. Hersman, the chairwoman of the safety board, noted: "We know that some people's lives were changed forever because of this accident."

So what caused it? Was there a mechanical error that led the ferry to accelerate instead of slowing down? No, the commission tasked with investigating the incident clearly stated that there were no mechanical issues that contributed to the crash. Was it perhaps a breakdown in communication? Bad processes? The incident report cleared those

---

4 Financial Services Commission of Ontario. "Minor Injury Guideline." Superintendent's Guideline No. 01/14, February 2014, *https://www.fsco.gov.on.ca/en/auto/autobulletins/2014/Documents/a-01-14-1.pdf*.

possibilities as well, and the captain passed all drug and alcohol tests. What was the cause, then? A very simple manipulation error, because of a design flaw in the control panel.

Earlier during the trip, the captain felt a vibration when passing near a bridge. Thinking that some debris might be caught in the propeller, he switched the piloting system to a backup mode that gave him manual control of the propeller blades. This is what is expected and is a usual procedure. However, he forgot to switch back to normal piloting mode. As the ferry reached the pier, the captain prepared the usual approaching maneuver. However, in backup mode, this manipulation creates an acceleration instead of a deceleration.

To further confuse the captain, the ferry had three piloting consoles: one on each side of the vessel and one in the middle. Following the usual approaching procedure, he transferred the control to the console on the right side so he could see the dock. When he realized that the ferry was not slowing down, he ran to the center console, thinking that he might have made a mistake when transferring the controls. But again, the ship didn't respond. In the seconds that he had before the crash, he ran from one control panel to another, without noticing that he had misdiagnosed the issue.

The captain was described by the investigators as conscientious and experienced. He was trained by the manufacturer and he had even trained other captains on this piloting system. However, regardless of this experience and training, we can understand how he could make such an error when looking at a picture of the console (see Figure 2-6).

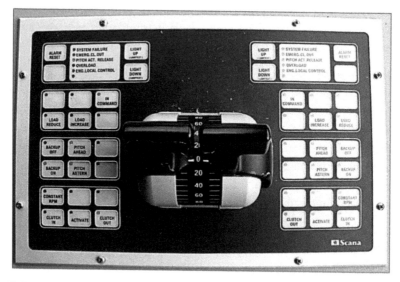

FIGURE 2-6.

The ferry's control console. How quickly can you spot the "backup on" button with its tiny indicator light among the mass of other buttons and possible modes? (source: National Transportation Safety Board)

Give yourself a few seconds to locate the "backup on" button with the indicator illuminated among the mass of other buttons and possible modes. Did you find it? No? Try again, it's on the left side. Are you able to tell if this console is in control, or if another one is? *When using modes as a design pattern, the interface should always clearly indicate every element that is affected by this mode.* Again, this ties back to Nielsen's first rule of usability:

1. Visibility of system status

   The system should always keep users informed about what is going on, through appropriate feedback within reasonable time.

USE APPROPRIATE VISUAL FEEDBACK

A tiny red dot is not appropriate visual feedback for such an important feature. A good example of appropriate feedback is the iPhone's home screen in "dancing" mode. When the user presses for a long time on the screen, the app icons start to wobble. This indicates that they can be dragged around and reorganized (see Figure 2-7). The user has switched to an "editing mode" from a "reading mode." The continuous animation helps the user to understand that a tap on an app icon will not yield the same result as usual. Also, every element of the interface that is affected by this mode—but only these elements—is behaving differently. The elements of the display that are not affected, such as the battery level, the clock, and the cell phone operator, are not behaving differently than usual.

In the case of the ferry control panel, the design was working against the pilot. The interface did a poor job of highlighting all the functions that were affected by the selected mode. A minor distraction was all it took to miss the small red dot that indicated a completely different output for the same action. Design should always do the work of preventing a mistake, reducing the user's cognitive load, instead of placing the burden on the user to avoid one. A sneeze, a bird flying by, a message on the intercom...these banalities shouldn't be sufficient to cause a fatal error. When a government report blames the design for the injury of 75 people, it's really bad!

FIGURE 2-7.

On iOS, shaking icons are a sign that the iPhone is in the mode that lets you move or delete apps

Case Study 3: Ford Pinto

In the late 1960s Ford was in heavy competition with foreign automakers to create an affordable subcompact car. The company set itself a lofty goal: its new car wouldn't weigh an ounce over 2,000 pounds and would not cost a cent over $2,000. This is what Ford considered its customers demanded. Winning in the subcompact market was a difficult endeavor. When consumers were searching for low-end cars, the price was a very important factor. Charging an extra $25 for a car could price you out of the market. This was the environment in which the Pinto (see Figure 2-8) was rushed to production in 1970. It sold very well for several years, as Ford was the second biggest automaker and considered a trustworthy choice. In the first few years, however, a number of incidents were reported where the cars would burst into flames when rear-ended, even at low speeds such as 20–28 mph! At slightly higher speeds the rear would crumple and the doors would jam, imprisoning the driver and any passengers while the car caught fire. The cause was a flaw in the design of the fuel tank and its placement, and it is known to have killed at least 180 people.

Obviously, you may not be working on cars, let alone on gas tanks. The reason we are highlighting this example is not to learn from the design errors, but from the process and reasoning that led to this car being manufactured and sold even though the issue of the gas tank placement had been identified before it went into production.

In the Pinto, the gasoline tank was located just underneath the rear bumper, behind the axle. When the car was hit from the back, the rear end would compact, causing the fuel tank to be pushed into other parts of the car. This would split the tank and allow fuel to leak out. Other times, the filler neck (the part you stick the nozzle into when filling up) would break off and the gas would spill out. The evaporating gasoline fumes would then surround the car and leak into the interior. At that point, all it needed was a spark to cause an explosion, which in a collision usually comes from metal friction or electrical wires shorting. Adding to the horror, the doors would jam, locking the unfortunate passengers inside. The engineers and designers working on the car placed the gas tank in the rear due to some very understandable factors. They could have placed it over the rear axle, which was standard for most subcompact cars, but that configuration created some engineering challenges with this car's design and also affected its center of gravity. Another option was to place it above the axle, but that would have taken up precious trunk space. Thus, they decided to put it under the car, near the back bumper.

FIGURE 2-8.
The Ford Pinto (image courtesy of Joe Haupt on Flickr)

An article in *Mother Jones* published in 1977 reported the comments of an engineer regarding the atmosphere of working at Ford during that time:

> "This company is run by salesmen, not engineers; so the priority is styling, not safety." He goes on to tell a story about gas-tank safety at Ford:

> Lou Tubben is one of the most popular engineers at Ford. He's a friendly, outgoing guy with a genuine concern for safety. By 1971 he had grown so concerned about gas-tank integrity that he asked his boss if he could prepare a presentation on safer tank design. Tubben and his boss had both worked on the Pinto and shared a concern for its safety. His boss gave him the go-ahead, scheduled a date for the presentation and invited all company engineers and key production planning personnel. When time came for the meeting, a grand total of two people showed up—Lou Tubben and his boss.

"So you see," continued the anonymous Ford engineer ironically, "there are a few of us here at Ford who are concerned about fire safety." He adds: "They are mostly engineers who have to study a lot of accident reports and look at pictures of burned people. But we don't talk about it much. It isn't a popular subject. I've never seen safety on the agenda of a product meeting and, except for a brief period in 1956, I can't remember seeing the word safety in an advertisement. I really don't think the company wants American consumers to start thinking too much about safety—for fear they might demand it, I suppose."[5]

Sound familiar in your organization? The engineers working on the Pinto were doing their best to meet the demands of the stakeholders and to raise concerns about the safety of their design. But the company as a whole was concerned about profits and sales.

In 1970, while the Pinto was in production, it was already known that rear-end collisions would cause serious fire hazards. By 1972 at least six additional crash tests had been done, at speeds ranging from 15 to 30 mph. Some were done on the current design and some with a modified design that included a small part added to damper the collisions. The tests showed that the modified design was effective in preventing or lessening the fuel leakage and preventing the explosion. The part cost between $5 and $11 and would make the car significantly safer. So the managers did a cost-benefit analysis. First, they estimated the cost of fixing the issue:

12,500,000 vehicles x $11 per car = $137,500,000

In order to calculate if the fix was economically viable, they had to come up with a price for not fixing it. They estimated that there might be 2,100 accidents, with 180 deaths and 180 serious burns. Then they used an estimate provided by a National Highway Traffic Safety Administration (NHTSA) report in 1972 to come up with a value for a life (see Figure 2-9).[6] In this report, a life was deemed to be valued at $200,000 (adjusted for inflation, in 2015 this would be around

---

5   Dowie, Mark. "Pinto Madness." *Mother Jones* (September/October 1977): 18–32. Available at *http://www.motherjones.com/politics/1977/09/pinto-madness?page=2*.

6   Birsch, Douglas, and John Fielder (eds.). *The Ford Pinto Case: A Study in Applied Ethics, Business, and Technology*. Albany, NY: State University of New York Press, 1994.

$1,200,000). Average compensation for a serious injury was estimated at $67,000. With this information, they calculated the cost of paying for the harm they would cause:[7]

(180 deaths x $200,000) + (180 burn injuries x $67,000) +

(2,100 burned cars x $700 per car) = $49,500,000

Ford projected a total cost of $137 million to fix the problem and a total cost of just $49.5 million to pay out the damages in litigation. The conclusion was that it would cost a lot more to fix the problem than to let it go and pay for any damage, so they decided not to fix it.

This sure seems like a heartless calculation. Why would a company make such a seemingly immoral decision? A student questioned the famous Nobel Prize–winning economist Milton Friedman about the principle behind this cost-benefit analysis (*https://youtu.be/ VdyKAIhLdNs*). When asked about the Pinto incident, Friedman responded with this question: "What if instead it had cost a billion dollars—should Ford have put the safety blocks in nonetheless?" He argued that Ford's approach to calculating the costs was a valid one, as "a matter of principle"—not that the numbers they used were the right ones, just that there are limited resources and every company has to put a price tag on a life in some decisions. This was the logic Ford used to make that decision, and the same logic has been used by many other companies before and since. This kind of thinking is obviously dangerous in its simplicity. It completely abstracts the concept of suffering from the equation. What's a life worth? Friedman's point is that we cannot claim each life has limitless value, because we would run out of resources for other lives that also have value.

---

7 Grush, E. S., and C. S. Saunby. "Fatalities Associated with Crash Induced Fuel Leakage and Fires." Internal Ford memo, available at *http://www.southerninjurylawyer.com/ media/2009/05/ford-memo.pdf*.

WHAT'S YOUR LIFE WORTH?

Societal Cost Components for Fatalities, 1972 NHTSA Study

COMPONENT	1971 COSTS
FUTURE PRODUCTIVITY LOSSES	
Direct	$132,000
Indirect	41,300
MEDICAL COSTS	
Hospital	700
Other	425
PROPERTY DAMAGE	1,500
INSURANCE ADMINISTRATION	4,700
LEGAL AND COURT	3,000
EMPLOYER LOSSES	1,000
VICTIM'S PAIN AND SUFFERING	10,000
FUNERAL	900
ASSETS (Lost Consumption)	5,000
MISCELLANEOUS ACCIDENT COST	200

TOTAL PER FATALITY: $200,725

FIGURE 2-9.

What's Your Life Worth? Expert table from a study used in the landmark case putting a cost on a human life.

While true, this way of thinking lulls us into feeling comfortable in crunching the numbers and making decisions like these. Also, it doesn't take into consideration other costs hidden in these catastrophes, such as bad press and loss of consumers' trust—both pretty significant costs, but harder to quantify. By deciding the variables to be taken into consideration in that business decision (life and value), Ford knowingly ignored other variables in their decision-making process (emotional cost, suffering, brand trust, employee distress, etc.). If the people tasked with making this decision at Ford had considered their customers' lives as something sacred, if they had had strong ethical principles, if they had listened to their engineers, they would have kept looking for more solutions. A questionable solution, but still better than not saying anything, would have been to let drivers make the choice. If they wanted to take the risk, fine. But if they weren't comfortable with it, they could have paid $11 more for their cars.

Here's another interesting point that offers a better perspective. Later, the engineers and designers actually did come up with additional ways to fix the issue: a block, a rubber bladder inside the gas tank, and a plastic insulator between the bolts and gas tank that cost less than $1.

Even after discovering these newer, cheaper, solutions, the car continued to roll off the lines unmodified, and as a result, some estimate that up to 180 people died in addition to 24 that were severely burned.[8] Actually, the numbers might be even higher since these are only the ones found in legal cases. Adding insult to injury, Ford lobbied against an automobile safety act. It delayed the bill for many years, which increased the perceived savings of its cost-benefit analysis. In the end, Ford's calculations were way off. The cost of litigation turned out to be much higher than expected. In a single case, Ford had to pay $3.5 million in damages to a boy who was severely burned and disfigured, while the driver in this accident had died. Ford quickly started settling out of court on every case, and eventually was forced to do a recall anyway to repair the 1.5 million cars that were affected. Ford's President later reflected:

> The [lawsuits] might have bankrupted the company, so we kept our mouths shut for fear of saying anything that just one jury might have construed as an admission of guilt. Winning in court was our top priority; nothing else mattered. And of course, our silence added to all the suspicions people had about us and the car.[9]

DIVERGING FROM THE ORIGINAL QUESTION

Oftentimes, what seems like a simple cost-benefit calculation with set variables is actually quite malleable. When facing a dilemma about implementing a costly fix or dealing with the consequences of not doing it, we must learn to diverge from the original argument. Instead of asking "Should we do it?" or "Is it worth it?" ask a different question:

---

8 Wojdyla, Ben. "The Top Automotive Engineering Failures: The Ford Pinto Fuel Tanks." *Popular Mechanics*, May 20, 2011, *http://bit.ly/2k4t6RS*.

9 Iacocca, Lee, and Sonny Kleinfield. *Talking Straight.* Toronto: Bantam Books, 1988.

"Is there a better solution?" *There is rarely a single solution to any problem.* Other solutions usually lie just under the surface. If Ford had had higher ethical standards and encouraged its employees to seek out solutions, they could have found those cost-effective fixes sooner, saved the company a lot of money, retained the brand's reputation, and most importantly saved lives.

Case Study 4: Flight 148

On the cold night of January 20, 1992, Air Inter Flight 148, commanded by Captain Christian Hecquet and First Officer Joël Cherubin, departed Lyon–Saint Exupéry Airport in Lyon, France. Both were experienced pilots with over 12,000 hours of flying between them. The quick flight to Strasbourg, Germany, catered to business travelers. The airline prided itself on short turnarounds with incentives to pilots for quick flights without delays. The plane was an Airbus A320 which could be programmed, even before takeoff, to land on a specific runway. On that night, during their approach, the control tower notified the pilots that they needed to land on a different runway because of adverse weather conditions. Planes' autopilot systems use radio signals sent by a beacon on the runway to provide precise navigational information. Unfortunately, the adverse weather and the mountainous terrain caused interruptions in these signals. The air traffic controller suggested they head to an alternate alignment beacon. The captain agreed, started to calculate the new descent approach for landing, and programmed the autopilot. He properly calculated a smooth descent angle of 3.3 degrees, which he entered into the instrument. He then made the final turn to align with the runway and beacon, corrected his direction, and initiated the landing sequence he had programmed in. The landing gear went down and the speed brakes on the wing went up. Everything was going according to plan, aside from some slight alignment issues, which they turned their attention to fixing. Suddenly the cloud cover broke and they came face to face with the mountain. Within a few seconds, the aircraft struck trees and impacted into an 826-meter-high (2,710 feet) ridge near Mt. Sainte-Odile.

Eighty-seven people died that day, and amazingly nine survived with injuries.

The investigation took a lot of time because the black box was charred beyond its engineered limit. But the investigators were eventually able to gather data from other recorders located in the front of the plane, as well as the voice data recorded. What they found was that as the aircraft was making its final turn the plane suddenly entered a very steep descent, about two and a half times the normal descent one would expect for landing. Without this steep descent, the plane could easily have cleared the mountain. The plane started the steep descent a whole minute before the impact, so why didn't the pilots spot it? The answer finally came when they discovered an interesting anomaly. On the voice recorder we hear the pilot say "a descent angle of 3.3," but the actual angle was 11 degrees. The investigators noticed that the vertical speed during the descent was 3,300 ft/min. There are two modes for descent: flight path angle (FPA) mode and vertical speed (VS) mode. A pilot can use either mode, but they require different units. When using a descent angle, it's entered as two digits with one decimal. For example, −3.3 would mean a descent angle of 3.3 degrees. When using vertical speed mode, the pilot enters the number of feet per minute that the plane should drop. In this mode, −3,300 ft/min is abbreviated to just −33. Looking at the display (see Figure 2-10), the only differences between the two modes are the presence of a decimal, and the small letters displayed above them. To make things worse, a plane's cockpit has hundreds of knobs, lights, controls, and displays. This makes this particular display even harder to notice (see Figure 2-11). In this fatal instance, the pilot forgot to push the mode selector knob before typing in "−33." He failed to see the mistake because the numbers are both displayed so similarly.

FIGURE 2-10.
Top: flight path angle mode; bottom: vertical speed mode (source: *http://bit. ly/2oxuGgY*)

FIGURE 2-11.
Position of the display in the Airbus 320 family cockpit (image courtesy of Ralf Roletschek, *http://www.fahrradmonteur.de*)

Once the landing sequence was initiated, that meant the airplane started to dive and picked up speed. It took just one minute for the plane to hit the mountain. With the cloud cover being so thick, the pilots would never have seen it coming. Any pilot would tell you that in a plane, it is difficult to tell if you are rising or falling, going fast or slow, especially in cloud coverage. Pilots rely heavily on their instrumentation and their interfaces to inform them of what is going on.[10] In this case, a small decision by the cockpit designer to use modes, which are known to be confusing to users,[11] and to display the two numbers similarly (seemingly to have the different measures fit the hardware of the two-digit display), cost the lives of 87 people. Once the design flaw was discovered, the risk for other planes of the same model became apparent. They all had to be fixed to avoid pilots making the same mistake.

Alternatives to Modes

It is not a coincidence that this is the third example of a mode causing an error. It shows how terrible these are for usability. In interface design, a *mode* is a setting in which the same user input produces different results than it would in a different setting. That definition alone raises important flags. In the physical world, it's really rare that the same input results in two completely different (and sometimes even opposite) results. As Jef Raskin, author of *The Humane Interface* (Addison-Wesley), noted:

> Modes are a significant source of errors, confusion, unnecessary restrictions, and complexity in interfaces. [...] "It is no accident that swearing is denoted by #&%!#$&," writes my colleague, Dr. James Winter; it is "what a typewriter used to do when you typed numbers when the Caps Lock was engaged."

Raskin is, understandably, very vocal about the dangers of using modes. He suggested "quasimodes" as an alternative. A quasimode is a state in which users must make some constant physical action in order to stay in that state. Therefore, they cannot forget that they are in that mode.

---

10 Johnson, Eric N., and Amy R. Pritchett. "Experimental Study of Vertical Flight Path Mode Awareness" International Center for Air Transportation, March 1995, *http://hdl.handle. net/1721.1/35913*.

11 See, e.g., Chapter 5 of Jakob Nielsen's book *Usability Engineering* (Morgan Kaufmann).

A good example would be the Shift key on a keyboard. It only changes the mode of input when it is physically pressed by the user, as opposed to the Caps Lock key, which often is activated by mistake or simply forgotten. This problem is so common that password fields now often add a "Caps Lock detector" (see Figure 2-12).

FIGURE 2-12.
WordPress login validation. When Caps Lock is detected on the WordPress login, the user gets a warning message.

In the case of a plane, it might be unrealistic for the pilot to physically hold down a button or a pedal in order to stay in a different descent mode. That could even contribute to causing other accidents. In this case, the interface should support and reinforce the mode it is in by using various types of feedback. A combination of a haptic and visual feedback could work in the case of the Caps Lock key. A mix of sound and visual feedback could be appropriate for cockpits. One thing is certain: a small text indication (that gets lost in a complex dashboard) is not sufficient.

Designing for Crisis Situations

In 2007, Cynthia stabbed her best friend 11 times, in an attempt to save his life. She had to do it, all because of a really, really poorly designed product. This is the reason she started getting interested by the subject of tragic design. Here's her story.

Before going to university, I spent all my money and a couple of months backpacking across Central America with my friends Val and Fred. We were on a journey to discover the world on a shoestring. At one point in Guatemala, in our quest to find all the hidden gems, we traveled to Rio Dulce to stay in a renowned hostel. This accommodation is built on *pilotis* on the river, and is not accessible by car; the only access is by boat.

In the morning, we ate breakfast and Val left for a swim. A couple of minutes later, Fred started feeling sick. Because he was wheezing, we thought it was asthma. But after giving him my own inhaler and seeing no improvement, I ran to the kitchen to verify the ingredients contained in the cereals we had had that morning. I quickly learned that they contained almonds. And...as you may have already guessed, Fred is very allergic to nuts. He was having anaphylaxis, which is a serious and life-threatening allergic response. In severe reactions, a person can go into shock, and if not treated immediately, it can be fatal.

Fortunately, he always traveled with his epinephrine injector. Epinephrine can save someone's life by relaxing the muscles around the airways, making breathing possible again. But it only works temporarily. After an injection, you have to seek medical attention immediately. Fred always told us that, should there be any problem, he had to be the one to inject himself. This always reassured me because I was quite intimidated by the idea of jabbing a big needle into my friend's leg. I handed Fred his Twinject injector, but, as the allergic reaction progressed, his hands started spasming and contracting. He was unable to hold the device and inject himself.

He gave me back the weird tube and I administered the first injection still sitting on the hostel's dock. I knew this would buy him some time, but we still had to get to a hospital, quick!

Ten awfully long minutes passed and we were finally on the boat on our way to the closest clinic. After all that time, Fred needed more epinephrine to keep his airway open until we reached medical help. Thankfully, the type of injector he traveled with was a Twinject, which has two doses. As we were speeding on the water, I tried to inject him with the second dose, but it didn't work. I tried again with no results.

I was trying to stay calm, but I couldn't figure this stupid thing out. I resigned myself to reading the long instructions that were glued and rolled around the tube (see Figure 2-13).

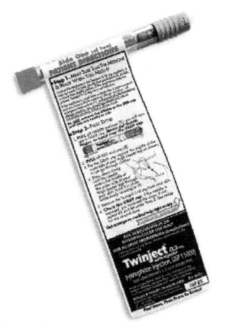

FIGURE 2-13.
Epinephrine injection pen. The first side of the instructions, rolled around the injector (source: *http://bit.ly/2oloVwz*)

I remember feeling so mad at myself for not being able to understand what they were instructing me to do. I read and redid all the steps, but couldn't make it work! I could still see the medication left in the transparent tube. Out of options, I stabbed Fred's thigh with the syringe. After 11 stabs, it somehow worked. To this day, I'm unsure why—I think that I simply broke it in his leg.

We reached the city a couple of minutes later, in time for Fred to receive adequate medical care. We left the hospital a couple of hours after. Fred was a bit shaken, had significant bruising on his thigh (due to my stabbing!), and was very tired, but he was alive. The outcome could have been different... things could have gone badly wrong because of a series of bad design decisions.

I now know, because I went on YouTube and looked for it, that all I had to do was to remove the little yellow piece at the end of the syringe (see Figure 2-14). It looks so simple in retrospect; I guess it always does after the fact. How could I miss such a simple instruction? Well, imagine the scene: we were going ridiculously fast, in a small, unstable boat. The water was bumpy and my hair was going crazy, whipping me in the face. Two tourists, who clearly didn't understand what was going on, were there with us in the boat, crying and freaking out. The boat driver yelled to me in Spanish, a language I had not mastered at that time, and on top of all that, I could hear Fred wheezing, asking one of the crying tourists to hold his hand.

Slide YELLOW collar off plunger.

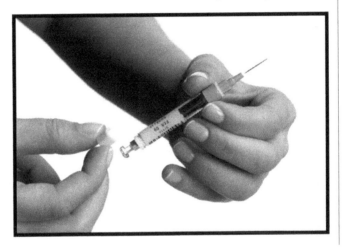

FIGURE 2-14.

The yellow collar that needs to be removed to allow for the second injection (source: *http://bit.ly/2n3Kk2D*)

For whatever reason, I couldn't find this collar. Maybe because it was yellow (the second color listed as a possibility for this piece), and in my hurry, I rushed through the text and missed that? Maybe because it was the ninth step on the double-sided instruction sheet, written in a very, very small font on paper that was flapping around because of the wind? Maybe because I was trying to read while calming my friend and dealing with the Spanish pilot who was also giving me instructions? Maybe because I thought that the plastic part was a design embellishment? Or maybe simply because, in such a stressful situation, I was freaking out and unable to follow complex instructions.

If I had wanted to save lives, I would have chosen a different career path. I could have become a police officer, a doctor, a nurse, or a paramedic…not a user experience designer. At least, that's what I thought before that day.

Every time I told this story before, I felt like I had to justify my inability to follow instructions. As if I needed to convince everyone that I'm not inherently stupid, like those actors in infomercials that can't peel an egg or use a can opener. However, as I was researching the subject, it quickly became evident that I was not the problem. According to one study on the use of the injector, "Half of the participants recalled incidents in which the EpiPen or Twinject did not work as intended or caused an injury."[1]

When half of the people using it misuse a product, we can confidently say that there's an issue with it. In the case of the injector, this issue can be resolved with better design. For example, making the collar's expected use more evident, ensuring the instructions were clear and simple (with images for the complex steps), and writing them in a bigger font would have helped me.

The dual-injector Twinject has since been discontinued. The newest generation of epinephrine injectors use prerecorded verbal messages directing the patient through usage. According to a study comparing the usability and patient preference of four different injectors, the talking ones significantly reduce the amount of errors in administration and are vastly preferred over the other nonspeaking injectors.[2] Aesthetics also play an important role in the design of these devices. One study points at the importance of the look of the device and its size, since its "weapon" resemblance makes it less likely to be carried around.[3] Literally making this object more attractive might save additional lives—isn't that exciting?

---

1 Guerlain S., L. Wang, and A. Hugine. "Intelliject's Novel Epinephrine Autoinjector: Sharps Injury Prevention Validation and Comparable Analysis with EpiPen and Twinject." *Annals of Allergy, Asthma & Immunology* 105 (December 2010): 480–484. doi:10.1016/j.anai.2010.09.028

2 Guerlain, Stephanie, Akilah Hugine, and Lu Wang. "A Comparison of 4 Epinephrine Autoinjector Delivery Systems: Usability and Patient Preference." *Annals of Allergy, Asthma & Immunology* 104:2 (2010): 172–177. doi:10.1016/j.anai.2009.11.023

See also Camargo, C. A. Jr., A. Guana, S. Wang, and F. E. Simons. "Auvi-Q Versus EpiPen: Preferences of Adults, Caregivers, and Children." *Journal of Allergy and Clinical Immunology: In Practice* 1:3 (2013): 266–272. doi:10.1016/j.jaip.2013.02.004

3 Money, A. G., J. Barnett, J. Kuljis, and J. Lucas. "Patient Perceptions of Epinephrine Auto-Injectors: Exploring Barriers to Use." *Scandinavian Journal of Caring Sciences* 27:2 (2013): 335–344. doi:10.1111/j.1471-6712.2012.01045.x

Fault Tree Analysis

When designing for a potentially risky scenario, there are tools that we can borrow from other fields to help us identify ways to reduce risk. Fault tree analysis (FTA) is one of them. Used in the aerospace, nuclear power, chemical, and pharmaceutical industries, this method helps us understand how systems can fail (*https://en.wikipedia.org/wiki/Fault_tree_analysis*). It's useful to come up with a list of potentially damaging situations and all of the factors leading up to these outcomes. Additionally it can be used as a diagnostic tool and help with the creation of a user manual. Fault trees are described by standards such as IEC 61025 (*https://webstore.iec.ch/publication/4311*); however, we suggest a simplified method that works for designers. The concept is quite simple: you start with an undesirable outcome and work your way back through everything that leads to that outcome. Let's use the dual injector from Cynthia's story to illustrate a fault tree (see Figure 2-15). One of the undesired outcomes with a dual injector would be:

(1) A patient dying from anaphylaxis on their way to the hospital.

Note that we always start with the worst outcome. We then work backward from this top event, and determine the ways that this could happen:

(1.1) Failure with the first dose

(1.2) Failure with the second dose

Branching from 1.1, we figure this could happen because of the following elements. We list them in order of likelihood of failure:

(1.1.1) The patient injects their hand instead of their leg

(1.1.2) The injector is broken

(1.1.3) The medicine is expired and thus ineffective

(1.1.4) The patient is physically unable to use the device

(1.1.5) The patient drops the injector and can't reach it

We then analyze the safety measures that are in place to prevent all of these from happening:

(1.1.1.A) The patient fails to see the word "Up."

(1.1.1.B) The patient fails to notice the blue color that should point at the sky.

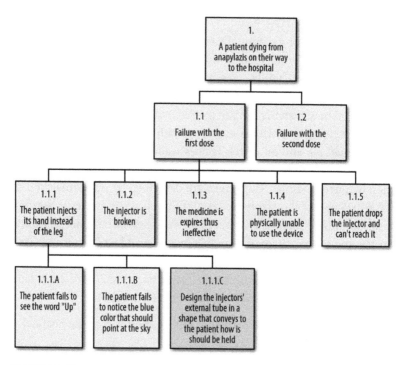

FIGURE 2-15.

Fault tree analysis of epinephrine injector. This simplified version of a fault tree can help in coming up with design requirements to reduce risk of harm

From this (rather simple) example, we notice that all the safeguards for this case are visual. We could add a design recommendation that would use another sense. For example: design the injector's external tube in a shape that conveys to the patient how it should be held. (How? Think of the way the handle of a saw or a knife makes it impossible to hold upside down.) We would then expand on 1.1.2, etc.

There are a multitude of risk analysis tools we can borrow from different disciplines. Other interesting ones include Root Cause Analysis (RCA) and Why-Because Analysis (WBA). These last two might be more appropriate as postmortem tools, to learn from incidents that have already happened.

Conclusion

Doing the right thing, putting users first, aiming for ethical excellence, and worrying about costs second turns out to be beneficial to companies. Apple has been a recent and grand example of this. As Steve Jobs,

Apple's CEO until 2011, famously said, "You've got to start with the customer experience and work back." When making the iPod, Apple took unprecedented care with the user experience: charging every device before shipping, spending more money on the packaging, and even polishing the inside of the case. All of this costs money, but customers can tell when care has been taken in creating products. Another example of this can be found in the Tesla Model S. In 2011, the NHTSA introduced tougher car safety standards. Tesla, being a brand new car maker, had a lot to learn. They could have aimed at making a car safe enough to pass all the tests and get the "5 stars in every category" seal of approval. Instead, they created the safest car ever tested, receiving a score of 5.4 out of 5, beating the next best car by almost double in a few categories.[12] That shows a commitment to their customers and to their craft. There is plenty of pressure for a young company in their position to turn profit for their investors.

We often give ourselves excuses when we choose to write off weak areas in our designs and products. We do some simple math and decide we don't have the resources for another revision. We should always challenge ourselves to improve those calculations—even more so when physical harm is a risk. We should always feel the pressure of the responsibility for those who put their lives in our hands. It could be your loved one's life, or even your very own. We should always treat it as such.

Key Takeaways

1. Bad design can cause physical harm or even death. Expressions like "minor injury" should be used with care, since they tend to downplay the seriousness of an incident.

2. Harm doesn't always come from negligence, but may come from bad processes and lack of usability standards or user testing.

---

12 Bartlett, Jeff. "Tesla Model S Aces Government Crash Test." *Consumer Reports*, August 21, 2013, *http://bit.ly/2niWIrP*.

3. Metrics are on the opposite end of the spectrum from empathy. They participate in stripping human beings of their personality and individuality.

4. Most accidents involving complex technologies are caused by a combination of many factors—organizational, managerial, technical, and even political. All software, even if extremely well designed, will behave in an unexpected way under certain conditions.

5. When it comes to medical interfaces, testing with real users in scenarios that are as realistic as possible is optimal.

6. When faced with a dilemma about implementing a costly fix or dealing with the consequences of not doing it, we must learn to diverge from the original argument. Instead of asking "Should we do it?" or "Is it worth it?" ask a different question: "Is there a better solution?" There is rarely a single solution to any problem.

7. Modes are terrible strategies for user interfaces. A design should instead use quasimodes, forcing the users to maintain some constant physical action in order to stay in that state. Therefore, they cannot forget that they are in that mode. If quasimodes are not appropriate, offer as many feedback types as possible: color, lights, sounds, haptic, etc.

Interview with Aaron Sklar

The following is an interview with Aaron Sklar, Managing Director of Experience Strategy and Design at Healthagen, and former IDEO designer.

1. How do you see bad design affecting healthcare?

As an industry, healthcare is rampant with examples of products and services that have been implemented with no regard for the doctors or patients who use them. There are many examples of breakthrough clinical technologies that provide amazing results for a health condition, yet few examples where anyone has taken the time to think through the user experience. Doctors' workdays are disrupted by intrusive digital tools that provide a functional service but in a way that makes the doctor's job laborious and unfulfilling. Similarly, most tools that are offered under the headline of "patient engagement" typically remove the opportunity for patients to have the experience of being cared for and understood.

2. How are you contributing to help solve it?

I have found time and again that our design team's contribution to health-care tools was received as a welcome refreshment worthy of celebration. I launched Prescribe Design (*http://www.prescribedesign.com*) as a way to celebrate designers who are making a difference in healthcare and to make the conversations about user experience in healthcare loud.

3. How did you find your way to designing for healthcare?

Most of my career has focused on healthcare design. There are so many areas in healthcare where design can make a powerful difference, that it has always been a very attractive opportunity to me as a designer.

4. How do you think design will be able to change healthcare?

The designer's superpowers are empathy and prototyping. Underlying both of these is a commitment to learning—learning about people's needs, learning through experimentation and trial, and arriving at a solution through iteration and discovery.

5. How can designers help?

Prescribe Design has articulated 12 core design challenges for healthcare (*http://prescribedesign.com/portfolio/northstar*). For each of these 12 challenges, we give examples of how we see designers playing a role.

Design Challenge #1 is "People should feel understood & cared for."

Design Challenge #5 is "Family caregivers should be acknowledged as credible members of care teams."

Design Challenge #7 is "Clinicians should be fulfilled by their work, and have the support they need."

6. How do you avoid designing something that will cause harm?

Piloting and prototyping are critical before scaling an intervention. Obviously, someone's health is not something to risk. Starting with simulation and small-scale prototypes will allow for learning and identifying unintended consequences.

7. What does that look like? How do you simulate users' actions before you try it out with real patients?

There is no right answer. One scenario of starting small is choosing a smaller population to start with. Depending on the type of novel intervention, I can imagine starting with the population of one small clinic, or perhaps a less at-risk set of patients.

8. What is the purpose of technology to you?

Great technology fades into the background. It's behind the scenes—not the hero. It helps get the job done faster or simpler, allowing people to create a more human interaction.

9. What is the biggest challenge when designing for healthcare?

There is systemic challenge in designing for healthcare. The financial and political systems make the delivery of health services and tools complex. Often things that seem like a no-brainer quick fix are harder than they look to execute on because of the complexity of the system behind the scenes.

10. What role does design have in making the world a better place to live?

When people understand that *someone* made a choice to have a product or service be the way it is, they start to recognize that we can also make changes to way things are. Designers are inherently optimistic.

11. What can designers add to their process in order to avoid causing harm in this way?

Building teams that represent and get input from all of the stakeholders involved. A design-driven solution may not take into account the medical reality. A doctor-driven solution may not take into account the cost to execute. A patient-driven solution may not take into account the complexity of the system. By bringing all of the stakeholders together, we can shape solutions that will work.

12. How do you balance the stakeholder needs when they are in conflict with one another?

When stakeholders are at odds with each other, the designer often takes on the role of facilitator/convener—again, showcasing empathy and prototyping as tools for creating alignment and consensus.

[3]

Design Can Anger

OF ALL THE WAYS we can hurt our users, emotional harm is the most common—and yet we often fail to detect it. This type of pain can't be seen on the outside, and it's dealt with in ways that differ greatly from one person to another. We won't read in the papers that "due to a change in the interface, 34 users have reported feeling angry." However, we will hear (a lot) about exploding cell phones that have injured customers (*http://bit.ly/2mp2334*). There is a multitude of ways design can cause pain. The effect can range from just making the user feel uncomfortable to full-on grief, heartache, misery, and even depression. Our products and designs might cause someone to feel all of those negative feelings, but the one we are the most familiar with is frustration. Why? Because we know that frustrated users mean lost customers, vocal detractors, and lower revenues. Companies tend to focus on converting unhappy customers into happy ones. But that line we draw is disingenuous and oversimplifies the situation. We usually consider our unhappy customers as "defective products" that need to be fixed, but when do we stop and take the time to actually consider what they are feeling?

In this chapter, we will explore why and how certain design decisions can anger our users. We know that there are many more reasons that this could happen, but we will focus on two culprits: impolite technologies and dark patterns.

Why Should You Care About Emotions?

But first, why should we care about different emotions? Research tells us that people are more impacted by a bad experience than a good one.[1] Therefore, if we want happy, paying customers, we are better off spending our time avoiding and fixing bad experiences. Emotional harm has a real impact on users, and it can't just be made right by a quick email, phone call, or reply on Twitter from our brand. We can see this in full effect on Yelp, the business review platform. Many users will give a restaurant a 1-star review because the server was rude, even if the food and ambience were great. Emotional harm should be taken very seriously.

Of all emotions, *anger* is the easiest to notice because it usually causes visible reactions. It's important to understand what causes the frustration our users experience. A natural reaction to pain or being hurt is anger. It's part of the instinctive nature of human beings. When the danger of being hurt is perceived (rightfully or not), the fight mechanism of anger helps to ensure protection. There are many steps that can be taken to prevent causing anger with the experiences we craft. One of the easier ways is to make sure your design is polite.

It might sound silly to propose politeness as a solution to anger. However, politeness serves as a way to establish a positive relationship between everyone involved in a situation and bridges the gap between different backgrounds. Politeness also contributes in reinforcing the relationship between humans and machines. As Brian Whitworth and Adnan Ahmad put it in *The Social Design of Technical Systems: Building Technologies for Communities* (The Interaction Design Foundation):

> Software, with its ability to make choices, has crossed the border between inert machine and social participant, as the term human-computer interaction (HCI) implies. Computers today are no longer just tools that respond passively to directions but social agents that are online participants in their own right. [If] I hit my thumb with a hammer I blame myself, not the hammer, but people often blame equally mechanical programs for user initiated errors.

---

1 Baumeister, Roy F., Ellen Bratslavsky, Catrin Finkenauer, and Kathleen D. Vohs. "Bad Is Stronger than Good." *Review of General Psychology* 5:4 (2001): 323–370.

Characteristics of Impolite Technologies

Let's explore what makes a technology impolite and what design solutions should be implemented to ensure politeness.

IMPOLITE TECHNOLOGIES ARE SELFISH

They push themselves forward at every opportunity. This is probably the most visible characteristic. In a real-life interaction, it is considered polite to ask your interlocutors about themselves before talking about you. The same applies to the software world. A tool should always put its users' needs before its own. Any piece of software that steals the focus from what the user is doing is automatically considered impolite.

Xbox's frequent updates

Periodically, when turning on an Xbox, the user has to wait for a software update. This update is "required" to load, even before the main screen comes up. The updates can be quite large and take a lot of time to download and install. Not only does the system check for updates before the user can play, but it also doesn't give any valid options to skip the update, or "snooze" it, if the user is in a rush, busy, or simply doesn't want to install it immediately. The user can either do the update, or turn off the device (see Figure 3-1). Even if Xbox could argue that the updates end up benefiting the user and are important, very often they are not essential right away.

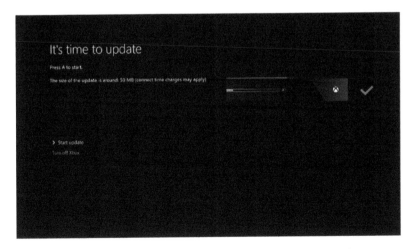

FIGURE 3-1.
The Xbox update screen shows up before the user can do what they intended to do, and doesn't let them choose to "snooze" the install

Google Calendar event reminders

If a user has an alert for an upcoming event, and their Google Calendar is open on a tab in the browser, it will steal the focus from the active tab to present a pop-up that needs to be dismissed (see Figure 3-2). This is extremely frustrating. In a work environment, people often have multiple meetings per day, and the fact that the Calendar steals the focus from what the user is doing creates an interruption. Some studies suggest that once interrupted, it can take a person up to 23 minutes to get back into a productive flow.[2] We understand that Google Calendar is trying to be helpful, but a notification that doesn't require an action and that is less disruptive would be much more polite.

FIGURE 3-2.

Google Calendar steals the focus from the active tab, and requires an action to dismiss the alert

---

2   Gregusson, Halvor. "The Science Behind Task Interruption and Time Management." Yast blog, May 23, 2013, *https://www.yast.com/time_management/science-task-interruption-time-management.*

IMPOLITE TECHNOLOGIES ARE LAZY

They require more effort from the user than necessary, while providing little value in return. Software, in opposition to human brains, is really good at remembering locations, settings, preferences, etc. It should use that strength to benefit users and unburden them of extra work.

For example, many phone applications require authorizations (e.g., permission to access the microphone or the phone's camera) to be used. What we often encounter is a dialog box that merely states that the user needs to go into their settings to change this permission. Why should the user have to find where they have to go to change the required setting? Why do they have to do the all the work? These mundane tasks should be performed by the software, not the user. Not only is it useless additional cognitive work, but it's also a waste of users' time. The app should always link to the right location in the settings. Facebook Messenger for iPhone does this really well (see Figure 3-3).

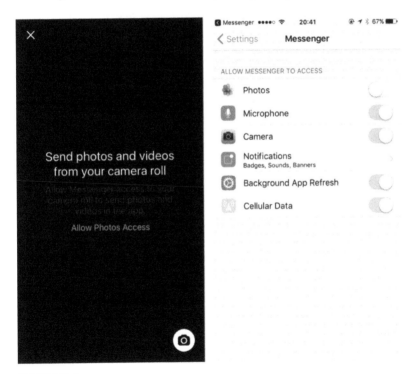

FIGURE 3-3.
Facebook Messenger permission dialog. When asking for permission to access the Camera Roll of your iPhone, the app links directly to the right place, making it easy for the user.

The following example is another illustration of laziness.

Self-checkout

Since their invention in the nineties, self-checkout machines are getting more and more popular (*https://en.wikipedia.org/wiki/Self-checkout*). The idea is simple. If the customer assumes the job of the cashier by scanning and paying for the items themselves, the retailer can save money on employee salaries. Retailers and self-checkout providers tend to dismiss criticism. They say that these machines allow for faster checkout while engaging actively with the customer. But tests performed by a journalist from CBC showed that not only does it take significantly longer for customers, but they also make more errors when checking themselves out:

> The cashier was able to get through the transaction faster and with fewer problems. And in one case, an incorrectly punched code at a self-checkout meant one shopper was charged $70 for 10 brussels sprouts.[3]

In addition to taking up more of the customer's time, the machines are extremely rude, yelling impolite instructions continuously. If a clerk were to bark "Unexpected item in the bagging area!" or "Remove your card!" repeatedly, they would receive complaints from customers. *Why do we allow machines to behave in a way we find unacceptable in a human?*

Finally, as with most impolite services, this technology ends up not being entirely beneficial to the company using it. Self-checkouts are so bad that grocery stores end up losing money with them. In a study performed by two criminologists from the University of Leicester in England,[4] we learned that self-checkouts in the US and various European countries have contributed to a financial loss of some 4%. Considering that the profit margin of the average grocery store is around 3%, this is catastrophic. The major driver of this loss is theft, often spurred by frustration:

---

3 Griffith-Greene, Megan. "Self-Checkouts: Who Really Benefits from the Technology?" CBC News, January 28, 2016, *http://bit.ly/2oEUwQ6*.

4 Beck, Adrian, and Matt Hopkins. "Developments in Retail Mobile Scanning Technologies: Understanding the Potential Impact on Shrinkage & Loss Prevention." University of Leicester, 2015, *http://bit.ly/2oF78a1*.

One in five people admit pilfering items at the checkout, but the results suggest people steal regularly once they realise they can get away with it—the majority admitting they first took goods because they couldn't work the machines.[5]

Another study confirms these findings. Of the population surveyed, nearly 20% of customers admitted to stealing at a self-checkout, and 60% of them said the reason was because they just couldn't get an item to scan.[6]

IMPOLITE TECHNOLOGIES ARE GLUTTONS

They are selfish about the device's limited resources, like a dinner guest who jumps on the cheese platter, leaving little to nothing for the rest of your company.

Gluttons run continuously in the background, stealing resources (data, bandwidth, RAM, space on the device, etc.). They sometimes play music or ads without a user-generated action. Other times, they perform heavy downloads and updates, making the internet/computer seem slow to users who don't know something is running in the background.

iTunes's silent downloads

iTunes, Apple's media library, quietly downloads purchases made on other Apple devices. For example, if you purchase a large HD movie on your Apple TV, it will try to download it on your MacBook. While the idea is to be helpful, it should never do this at the expense of other software that is active. Obviously, this is an option that can be deactivated, but this requires work from the user. First they have to figure out that iTunes is the reason their internet connection seems slow, then they have to work out how to locate and configure this option.

Every update, sync, and download should happen during idle time, unless the user consciously chooses otherwise.

---

5 Carter, Claire. "Shoppers Steal Billions Through Self Service Tills." *The Telegraph*, January 29, 2014, *http://bit.ly/1UszoFc*.

6 Ryan, Tom. "Self-Checkout Theft Is Habit Forming." RetailWire, May 19, 2014, *http://www.retailwire.com/discussion/self-checkout-theft-is-habit-forming*.

IMPOLITE TECHNOLOGIES ARE ATTENTION FREAKS

Similar to a three-year-old, they feel free to interrupt the user at any time, announcing and demanding things. Almost every website we visit these days screams, "Sign up to our newsletter!" Unfortunately, they do this before we even have the chance to read their content and get interested in actually signing up. "Would you like to vote?" ask our apps, in the middle of our workflow. Dialog boxes interrupt with "You've been selected to answer a survey" while we're visiting an ecommerce website to compare products. Do we need more examples? These behaviors are worthy of reprimands when observed in a child, yet again, we blindly accept them from our technologies.

CASE STUDY: MICROSOFT OFFICE ASSISTANT

One infamous example of impolite software is the Office Assistant, also known as Clippy, that was introduced in Microsoft Office for Windows 97. The paperclip was an intelligent user interface that would assist users in completing different tasks. For example, when users typed the word "Dear" in a document, Clippy would pop up and offer its help to write a proper letter (see Figure 3-4). Despite the fact that it was based on solid research on social responses to computer technologies, and built by a competent team that did a lot of user testing, this feature turned out to be a complete failure (*http://xenon.stanford. edu/~lswartz/paperclip/paperclip.pdf*). It was so unpopular that its removal was used by Microsoft, on their home page, to sell Office XP! (See Figure 3-5.)

FIGURE 3-4.

Clippy the Office Assistant in Microsoft Word (source: *https:// en.wikipedia.org/wiki/ File:Clippy-letter.PNG*)

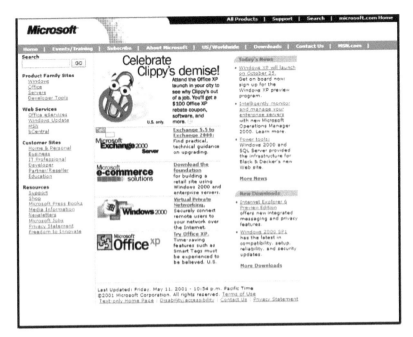

FIGURE 3-5.
Microsoft home page, circa 2001. Microsoft using Clippy's demise as a sales pitch for Office XP (source: *http://imgur.com/QdfrzKZ*).

There are many reasons why this technology ended up being disliked by so many. It was simply impolite. First, it would push itself forward, regardless of the task being accomplished. It demanded attention at every turn. When the user was writing a document, the software would interrupt to offer help, which would distract them from their train of thought. Second, it didn't respect the user's preferences. Hiding it repeatedly would not deactivate it, and even if a user permanently hid it in Word, it would pop up again the minute another program from the Office suite was opened. Lastly, the Office Assistant was optimized for the first use. It was perhaps amusing the first time it was encountered, but frustrating after that. It kept repeating the same things to the user, as if they were unable to understand the first time.

The key to all of this is imagining how a user would feel if, instead of an interface, they were dealing with a real person. Would this dialog be appropriate? Would it be absurd to ask these questions again? Google did a very funny commercial called "Google Analytics in Real Life" showing what ecommerce checkout experiences would be like for users if they were done in real life (*https://youtu.be/3Sk7cOqB9Dk*). All the interactions are recognizable from many online interfaces, such as having to remember your username, read a CAPTCHA, and deal with tricky add-ons. But putting the same experiences into a real-life scenario—in Google's commercial, it's buying a simple loaf of bread at a supermarket—puts into stark contrast the absurdities and impoliteness which are so common in our digital experiences. So next time you're designing this kind of interface, ask yourself, "What would this look like if the user were interacting with a real person?"

POLITE TECHNOLOGIES

In comparison, *polite* software would do the following:

1. Ask for the user's permission to perform an action.

   This one is very straightforward, yet failure to implement it is still one of the most frequent complaints from users. Before running an update, tracking usage, sharing the user's information, or setting itself as a default, an application or software should always ask for the user's permission in plain and explicit language. Avoid using double-negative formulations that are confusing ("uncheck if you do not wish to..."). Performing an action without the user's consent, even if it's meant to be good for the user, is impolite and dangerously close to what dark patterns do (we will discuss dark patterns later in this chapter). A great example of asking permission, even if the action would end up benefiting the users, is the app Chrome. When first installed, it asks the user for approval to send crash reports and usage statistics to Google (Figure 3-6).

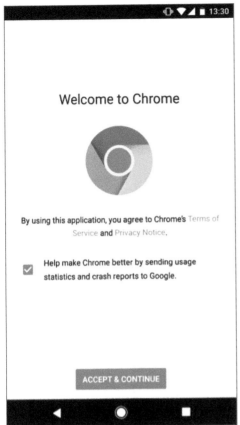

FIGURE 3-6.
Chrome crash reports
permission screen.
When first installed,
it asks the user for
permission to send
crash reports and
usage statistics to
Google.

2. Offer alternatives.

Announcing that your tool will perform an action is a good thing. However, solely announcing it is not sufficient: your dialog should give the user the choice to perform the action or not. One big culprit of announcing without offering alternatives is the application update. When one is required, it doesn't always let the user snooze the action that will prevent them from accomplishing the task they initially wanted to do. If the update is required for security and performance purposes, users should be offered the alternative to perform it later, during the night for example (Figure 3-7).

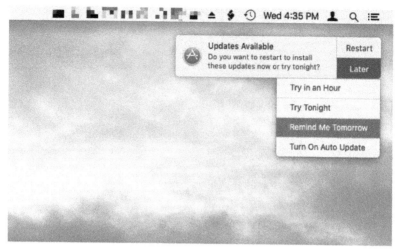

FIGURE 3-7.
App Store update reminder. The reminder allows users to update at a more convenient time.

3. Explain all of the options and settings.

   Not only should all the possible options and settings be explicit, but they should also offer sufficient information for any user to be empowered to make the right decision (Figure 3-8).

FIGURE 3-8.
QuickBooks online settings page. Some fields have additional text that helps users make the right decision.

4. Anticipate the user's need when possible.

   In a restaurant, a waiter refilling a glass of water before being prompted to is considered polite. The same should apply to your design. For example, a website can anticipate that someone shopping from a different country might appreciate a different language or different currencies. Another good example is the "Did you mean" feature of the search engine Google. When typing a popular request with a typo, the search engine will offer to search for the correct spelling (see Figure 3-9).

FIGURE 3-9.
"Did you mean" feature in Google Search. When you enter a common request with a typo, the search engine will offer to search for the correct spelling.

5. Respect (and remember) the user's decision.

There's a difference between anticipating users' needs and forcing decisions on them. For example, if a Canadian is visiting an American ecommerce site, it's convenient and polite to offer them the choice to use the Canadian dollar as currency or to point them at the Canadian version of the store, if there is one. However, if the visitor refuses, the website should not prompt them again on the next page or at the next visit. Also, the technology should trust that users are making their choices deliberately. Asking them to confirm every action twice is simply insulting. Unless the consequences of the user-generated action are irreversible, it should trust that the users know what they are doing. Amazon.com does something very clever: it reminds Canadians that they can shop on Amazon.ca in a pop-up the first time they visit the website, and indicates how many times they will show the reminder again, unless prompted not to (see Figure 3-10).

FIGURE 3-10.
"Shopping from Canada?" pop-up from Amazon.com. It indicates how many times the message will be shown again, unless prompted to stop.

6. Be mindful of words and tone.

    When encountering a dialog that asks, "Are you sure you want to quit without saving?" it's almost impossible not to read it with a very paternalistic tone ("Are you *sure* you want to quit without saving?"). It can be difficult to strike a balance between helpful instructions and patronizing ones. If it sounds like something an adult would say to a teenager, then reconsider the tone. Avoid sounding patronizing by reducing the use of the second person in your instructions. Addressing the user directly can work well, but try not to have two "yous" in the same sentence. This is even more important in some other languages, where the use of the second person singular pronoun is extremely informal (*http://bit.ly/2o7jZAe*). Ask permission to help before giving advice or a helping hand, regardless of your motives. Unsolicited help can seem patronizing and condescending. If you must jump in without asking, offer the critical reason why beforehand (see Figure 3-11). Also, be helpful in a way that the user will value. *Don't treat people the way you want to be treated. Treat people the way they want to be treated.*

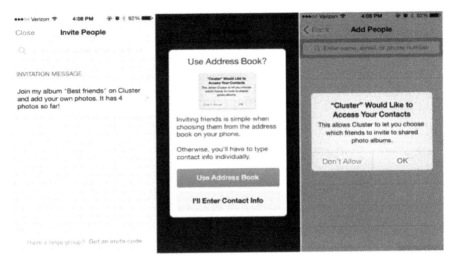

FIGURE 3-11.

Cluster onboarding. Before permission is requested, users are primed with why the access will be needed.

7. Bonus tip: fake politeness if necessary.

It has been shown that even faked politeness works well. A team of researchers found that a word-guessing game was rated as more enjoyable when the software would apologize after a wrong answer by saying "We are sorry that the clues were not helpful to you" instead of simply stating "Wrong answer."[7] It's a good practice to *put the blame on the situation instead of blaming the user* for an error. Also, formulations like "we are sorry to see you go" after a user has unsubscribed from a newsletter work well. Keep in mind that these lines must not be guilt-inducing. Therefore, placing them after the user has performed the action (e.g., unsubscribing) is more polite than placing them before the user has made their decision. MailChimp's login page is a good example of an interface blaming the situation, not the user (Figure 3-12).

---

7 Whitworth, Brian, and Tong Liu. "Politeness as a Social Computing Requirement." In
   Handbook of Conversation Design for Instructional Applications, edited by R. Luppicini.
   Hershey, PA: Information Science Reference, 2008. Available at *http://brianwhitworth.
   com/polite2.pdf.*

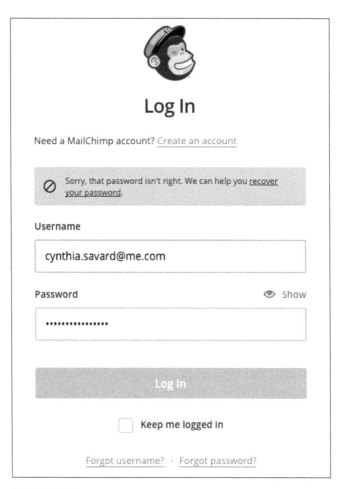

FIGURE 3-12.
MailChimp's password error message. The message indicates that they are "sorry" that the password isn't right; this is a polite variation from the usual "wrong password, try again."

Dark Patterns

There are times when our designs annoy users. We frustrate them when they try to cancel our services or unsubscribe from our marketing emails, or have trouble navigating to the information they need. Who hasn't felt like yelling out loud and throwing their phone on the couch (or the ground!) after trying to log into a government service or complete an online form for an insurance company? These small moments can seem harmless in isolation, but compounded (think of all the time a user spends interacting with technology!) they can be emotionally draining. While most frustrations are caused by ignorance of good design practices, other are intentionally designed to be complex. Many of the worst offenses have been identified by the UX community as "dark patterns," a term coined by Harry Brignull. This is how he describes them:

> A dark pattern is a user interface carefully crafted to trick users into doing things they might not otherwise do, such as buying insurance with their purchase or signing up for recurring bills. Normally when you think of "bad design," you think of the creator as being sloppy or lazy—but without ill intent. Dark patterns, on the other hand, are not mistakes. They're carefully crafted with a solid understanding of human psychology, and they do not have the user's interests in mind.[8]

They happen when a company values its business needs at the expense of its users' needs. Sometimes disguised as "growth hacking" initiatives, they are everywhere, used by even the best companies. If you have not been asked to design one in your career, then you surely have come across them as a user. There are many different types of dark patterns, but we selected the most common categories for this book. Feel free to visit *DarkPatterns.org* for more examples.

1. BAIT AND SWITCH

Bait-and-switch dark patterns happen when the user agrees to something, but something else (something undesirable) happens instead. The name comes from the fraud scheme where retailers advertise a certain product at a low price, but when the customer comes to buy it, they find that the product is not available or they are being sold something of lower quality. It's generally illegal.

There are many, many examples of this. A very common one is iPhone apps that want their users to give them good reviews on iTunes. Instead of simply asking, "Would you like to review our app?" they hide the action under a question like "Do you like cupcakes?" If the user clicks "yes" they are automatically directed to iTunes to give the app a review. Another common example is websites that want the user to sign up for

---

8   Brignull, Harry. "Dark Patterns: Inside the Interfaces Designed to Trick You." *The Verge*, August 29, 2013, *http://bit.ly/1fjQdvy*.

their marketing emails. They ask, "Would you like a discount code?" If the user supplies their email address, they actually sign up for the site's newsletter instead of getting a coupon. The users are baited into giving away their personal information.

Windows recently made the news with a change to its free upgrade pop-up. While in the previous version, when the user clicked the close button (the red "x" in the corner of the box) the pop-up was dismissed, as expected, in the newest version, clicking that button *agrees* to a scheduled upgrade rather than rejecting it (see Figure 3-13). According to the BBC, who wrote about this dark pattern, "This has caused confusion as clicking the cross typically closes a pop-up notification."[9] No kidding! That's so obvious, no one should have to write an article about it!

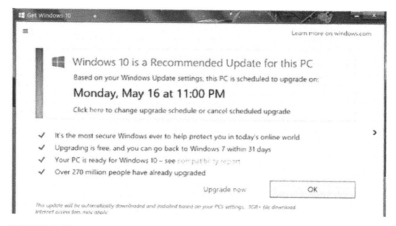

FIGURE 3-13.
Microsoft Windows 10 upgrade pop-up. Clicking the "x" schedules the upgrade instead of dismissing the dialog box.

Should you find out that your company is using this technique, there are many creative and effective ways to be honest, yet convincing. First, try working with a great copywriter. Be creative, without hiding any subsequent steps. While it's acceptable to use inspiring words in a call to action, make sure the users understand what the next steps are. For example, if a home decoration app were to use "Get inspired!" on a call to action that sends the users to its website's image gallery of

---

9   Kleinman, Zoe. "Microsoft Accused of Windows 10 Upgrade 'Nasty Trick.'" BBC News, May 24, 2016, *http://www.bbc.com/news/technology-36367221.*

user-generated home decors, that would be acceptable. "Get inspired!" on a call to action that would automatically download the app would not be.

2. FAKE CONTENT

This strategy has been used for a very long time in traditional marketing. Often referred as "native advertising," it consists of disguising advertising in the form of content *without proper indication*. This has become so common on websites that we've observed users starting to ignore legitimate articles because they are placed in a section that often contains ads.

The second version of this pattern happens when a fake button hides an ad. Do you remember the free software websites where there were three or four download buttons and you had to guess which one was the good one? This was such a big problem that you could find blog articles teaching users how to find the legitimate download button! (See for example Adam Kujawa's post,[10] source of the image in Figure 3-14.) Thankfully, Google has started to block websites that use these techniques (see Figure 3-15), calling them "deceptive."[11]

10 Kujawa, Adam. "Pick a Download, Any Download!" Malwarebytes Labs, October 19, 2012, *https://blog.malwarebytes.com/cybercrime/2012/10/pick-a-download-any-download/*.

11 Ballard, Lucas. "No More Deceptive Download Buttons." Google Security Blog, February 3, 2016, *https://security.googleblog.com/2016/02/no-more-deceptive-download-buttons.html*.

FIGURE 3-14.
Screen capture from a web service called Sendspace. Which one is supposed to be the right download button?

FIGURE 3-15.
Warning in the Chrome browser. This is what users will see when clicking on a link to a website that presents a fake download button.

3. FORCED CONTINUITY

Forced continuity happens when a service requires the user to enter their payment information in order to get a free trial. After the trial period is over, the user is automatically billed for the recurring service *without proper warning.*

Instead of applying this scheme, designers should suggest a foot-in-the-door (FITD) approach.[12] FITD is a compliance technique that consists of convincing someone of the benefit of something small, on the grounds that they are more likely to accept something slightly bigger after. This is an acceptable (and legal) selling technique. For example, ask your users to sign up for your newsletter, then offer them a free trial, then ask them to take out a monthly subscription, then sell them an upgrade to a larger plan, etc. For all of these requests, make sure you honestly disclose the price and the benefits. You could also use the reciprocity technique: if you give your users something valuable for free, they are more likely to purchase from you after!

4. FRIEND SPAM

The friend spam pattern occurs when a company harvests the contacts of a user to invite them to its service. It usually requires just a single click from users, who don't realize they are authorizing the app to send an email on their behalf to all of the people on their contact list. We all hate this pattern. Dark patterns tend to make the user feel stupid about being tricked, but this one amplifies that reaction by making them look stupid to all their friends too!

Here's Jonathan's personal experience with LinkedIn, the business-oriented social network, friend spamming on his behalf:

> I will never forget how I felt when LinkedIn tricked me into inviting everyone on my Gmail contact list to join. Gmail adds to this list anyone that you've ever emailed—so it sent invitations from me to everyone I had emailed since I first created my email account five years prior. It was terrible! My contacts included old teachers, customer service representatives, business contacts, extended family, and many others who did not appreciate the spam it sent out on my behalf. *I felt embarrassed and betrayed.* When the site asked me if I wanted to invite friends from my Google contact list, I thought I would be able to scroll through and mark off those I wanted to invite. Instead, once I gave it permission to access my list, it blasted the email to everyone. That was more than six years ago, and I still remember it. *LinkedIn has a big hill to climb in gaining my trust back.*

---

12 Freedman, Jonathan L., and Scott C. Fraser. "Compliance Without Pressure: The Foot-in-the-Door Technique." *Journal of Personality and Social Psychology* 4:2 (1966): 195–202.

5. MISDIRECTION

Misdirection is the magician's best trick. It's a form of deception where the performer focuses the attention of the public on one thing, in order to distract them from something else happening. The same happens in some interfaces, where design elements are used to distract the user from something else. While it's totally acceptable for a magician to use this deception technique on us (after all, we are paying to be deceived by a magician!), it's not what we would expect from a service, a website, or an app.

One of our favorite examples is the truck rental company U-Haul. On the company's website, people can reserve trucks. They are advertised for as low as $20, but as you go through the reservation process you end up unwittingly adding a bunch of add-ons if you're not paying attention (see Figure 3-16). Users can skip this step if they don't need any of these extras, but the design of the big yellow "Add these supplies" button is so misdirecting that it's actually hard to spot the "Clear all" link in the upper-right corner, or the diminutive "No thanks" option below it. The second offense on this website happens in the cart summary. Instead of showing you the actual total, it shows you what is "due today." This means that you have to pay more later, which is absolutely not clear if you don't get a calculator and do the math yourself (see Figure 3-17).

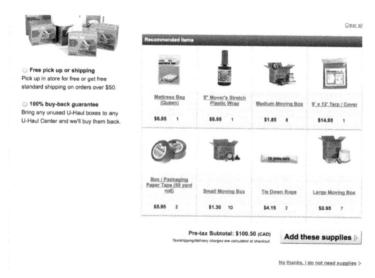

FIGURE 3-16.

One of the reservation steps from UHaul.com that automatically adds items to your cart. Notice the default values are all above 0.

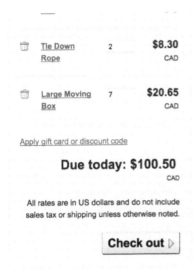

| | Tie Down Rope | 2 | **$8.30** CAD |
| | Large Moving Box | 7 | **$20.65** CAD |

Apply gift card or discount code

Due today: $100.50
CAD

All rates are in US dollars and do not include
sales tax or shipping unless otherwise noted.

Check out ▷

FIGURE 3-17.
Snippet of the cart summary on UHaul.com. The "Due today" total is
misleading and doesn't let the user know that there will be more to pay later.

6. ROACH MOTELS

One common dark pattern, notoriously used by Comcast and AOL,[13] is
called "The Roach Motel," where it's easy to sign up but hard to cancel
the service. The company intentionally makes the cancellation process
difficult and frustrating in the hopes that you will abandon trying to
cancel it, or put it off until later and forget about it. This pattern is very
often used with *forced continuity,* making this combination extra nasty
to the user.

Companies using this pattern tend to attract a lot of negative publicity
on social media. The technology podcast "Reply All" from Gimlet Media
recently did a whole segment on the home cleaning service Handy.com.
Handy let users subscribe to a recurring service online, but made it
impossible to cancel from the same website. To make things worse, not
only did users have to call to cancel, but the phone number was almost
impossible to find. Here's a quote from that episode (*https://gimlet-
media.com/episode/33-isis/*). The host, Alex Goldman, talks about his
experience trying to find the phone number:

---

13 See for example *http://bit.ly/1CACWHR* and *http://nbcnews.to/2mEPG3y.*

So it says, how can I contact Handy? We're here to help! "Contact us here," and it takes you to the help center and then, underneath it it says: "Still need help? Contact us." And there's another link. And that link takes you to the same place. Finally, after a bunch of Googling, I found this page that said: "To completely deactivate your regularly scheduled cleaning service: contact us." And I was stoked beyond belief and I clicked through and it takes you to the help center.

When we tried searching for others who had had the same issue, we found hundreds of tweets from unhappy customers. This is typically not the type of publicity a company is looking for. To its credit, Handy has listened to the criticisms and has since changed its website to offer a simple way to cancel the service. You no longer have to call, and the cancellation option is easy to find.

BONUS: TRICK QUESTION

This pattern is probably our favorite because of how absurd it is. Have you ever heard the motto, "If you can't convince them, confuse them"? This is what some services do to spike their metrics and get users to do something practically against their will, by using double negatives or inverting the usual expected behavior of interface elements. One of the best examples of a trick question is Royal Mail's newsletter registration form (see Figure 3-18). We suggest you take a moment to carefully read the information.

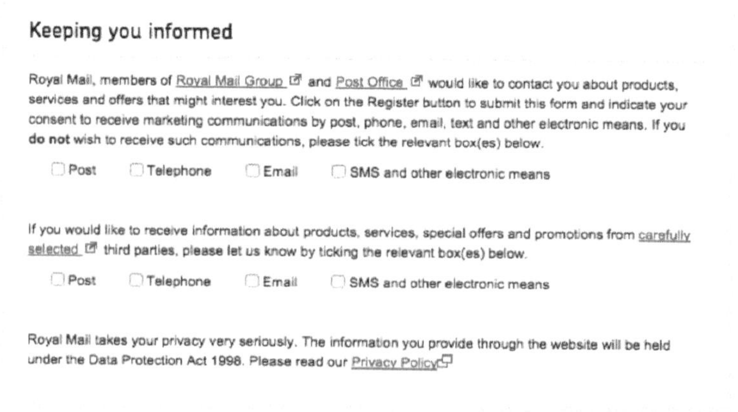

Keeping you informed

Royal Mail, members of Royal Mail Group ☐ and Post Office ☐ would like to contact you about products, services and offers that might interest you. Click on the Register button to submit this form and indicate your consent to receive marketing communications by post, phone, email, text and other electronic means. If you do **not** wish to receive such communications, please tick the relevant box(es) below.

☐ Post   ☐ Telephone   ☐ Email   ☐ SMS and other electronic means

If you would like to receive information about products, services, special offers and promotions from carefully selected ☐ third parties, please let us know by ticking the relevant box(es) below.

☐ Post   ☐ Telephone   ☐ Email   ☐ SMS and other electronic means

Royal Mail takes your privacy very seriously. The information you provide through the website will be held under the Data Protection Act 1998. Please read our Privacy Policy☐

FIGURE 3-18.
Screen capture from RoyalMail.com. The form asks users to check boxes to opt out on the first row, but to opt in on the second row. Now that's confusing!

The first row asks you to tick the boxes if you *do not* wish to receive marketing material. The second row asks you to tick the boxes if you *do* want to receive it. The normal pattern would be to leave all boxes unchecked, but this would subscribe you to all of the newsletters (inverting the expected behavior of a checkbox). If you were to read the first paragraph carefully, you'd realize that you have to check all the boxes to unsubscribe (double negation), but you would end up still registering to receive all the third-party newsletters because of the second instruction. If you are confused right now, imagine someone who is not aware of these dark patterns. There is no way they would get this right. Imagine any professional speaking to you that way in a real-life setup—you'd probably burst into laughter:

> Banker: Thanks for opening an account with us today! Would you *not* like to get insurance on it?
>
> Customer: Euh... yes?
>
> Banker: Okay. Are you *not* sure?
>
> Customer: Um...

Royal Mail recently updated their form. While we salute that they have removed the second question, they unfortunately kept the confusing wording on the first instruction.

THE DRAWBACKS

Why are these design tricks so easily found everywhere if they are so laughably bad? These dark patterns are prevalent because they work rather well at spiking conversion metrics. Forcing everyone who visits a site to sign up for a newsletter will increase subscriptions for this quarter, but is it really beneficial?

It can cost your company money

Some of these patterns have become illegal. For its friend-spamming strategy cited above, LinkedIn was fined $13,000,000 in a 2015 class action lawsuit.[14] Also, in Canada, there is now a law on spam and electronic threats that makes it illegal for companies to use opt-out check-

---

14 Roberts, Jeff John. "LinkedIn Will Pay $13M for Sending Those Awful Emails." *Fortune*, October 5, 2015, *http://fortune.com/2015/10/05/linkedin-class-action*.

boxes for newsletters and makes it mandatory to offer a simple way to unsubscribe. In September 2016, Kellogg Canada was fined $60,000 because of an email sent to people without their consent (*http://www. crtc.gc.ca/eng/archive/2016/ut160901.htm*); for the same offense but at a different scale, the airline Porter was fined $150,000 and the telecommunication company Rogers Media had to pay $200,000 (*http:// fightspam.gc.ca/eic/site/030.nsf/eng/00323.html*). We can only imagine that these cases of companies being sued for similar breaches will become more prevalent in the future.

It will hurt other metrics

This kind of design betrays the users' trust, for a short-term gain. It is wrong and a bad business strategy in the long run. Designing with a single metric in mind usually has negative consequences. For example, using a dark pattern to sneakily add items to users' shopping carts might seem like a good way to raise the average cart amount. However, when looking at the metrics before and after the implementation of the pattern, we realize that it's likely to hurt more than help. We call this the "zoom out" technique. Here are some of the results you might observe:

1. Lost opportunity to actually sell the real benefits of your products: if presented attractively enough, potential customers might have added them to their carts on their own.

2. The tricked customers might ask for more returns, increasing the return shipping costs and reimbursement costs.

3. They might contact you more over the phone, adding to the load of customer support calls and requiring more resources.

4. They might complain over social media. This can hurt your reputation, which is really hard to put a number on.

5. These customers won't become recurring customers and won't recommend your service to their friends and family; you will have to spend more on marketing to attract new customers, etc.

WINNING THE ARGUMENT

As designers, we stand between the business and the users, negotiating the interaction between them. We are in a unique position to advocate for our users and stand against bad design, for the good of the users and the business. When asked to design in this way or to disregard frustrations as "edge cases," we must stand up for users.

Taking a stand is not always easy. We suggest offering creative alternatives or advocating using persuasive design patterns to achieve better results in an ethical way. If this doesn't work, use the "zoom out" technique explained above. If this is still not sufficient, present some counterexamples (LinkedIn is always a good example because almost everyone has been friend-spammed by it).

Building a Case

Here's Jonathan's personal experience with implementing a dark pattern and building a case against it.

I remember the first time I was asked to implement one of these tricks. I love designing credit card forms; they are my favorite part of the customer conversion flow. So I was tasked with redesigning our checkout process. I read up on all the best practices, and after the project was over we saw a 12% increase in conversions! It was a win for the whole design team. On the tail of that success, we began to iterate some more. The VP of Marketing wanted to try implementing a few changes. We offered a 14-day free trial. We also offered a discount for the purchase of an entire year of our service. The unpleasant request I received was to hide the up-front cost by highlighting the free trial and concealing the fact that we would be charging for the full year rather than the calculated monthly equivalent we were displaying. So users would see a free trial, after which they would only be charged what seemed like a discounted monthly rate. However, when the two weeks of the free trial were finished, they got hit with a large charge for all 12 months (a couple hundred bucks).

I objected to implementing the design and gave my case, but the VP didn't budge and decided to go ahead with it anyway. Sure enough, revenue spiked after the change and it seemed as if he was vindicated. But I still didn't feel right. We weren't doing right by our customers. So I set out to dig deeper, to see if there was a hidden cost and prove that it was hurting our users as well as the company. My contacts in the customer support team told me they were overwhelmed; they'd had a huge spike in cancellations and support calls and needed to hire more staff. I was even able to listen in on calls for an hour and hear the frustration in our customers' voices—they felt cheated, many were livid. I gathered the support metrics, paired them with our weekly satisfaction numbers, and even showed how in the week of my investigation revenue had already begun to dip. I presented these facts to the VP of Marketing, and his eyes lit up. He was sold. I was speaking his language: metrics, data, business goals. A light bulb also went on in my head: discover what language the people you work with speak. What do they value? How do they see the world?

From that moment on the design team went from a team that "made things look pretty" to a data-driven team that added major value to the company. *Over time, we proved that treating users with respect always pays off in the long run.* Looking back, knowing what I know now, I wish our team had decided earlier what our values and principles were, so when the time came we had known that was crossing the line. I also wish I had started earlier in developing my relationship with that VP, and understanding his "language." I now make sure my values are aligned with my team's, and when possible with those in leadership's as well.

PERSUASION IS NOT DECEPTION

It's important to note that dark patterns are *not* acceptable selling or marketing techniques. The solutions we suggest are *persuasive design strategies*. These are all very acceptable ways to convince users to subscribe to or purchase your product. As explained by Anders Toxboe:

> You aren't going to convince people they want something that they would otherwise not be interested in. Persuasion must be honest and ethically sound to continue its effect beyond just a brief encounter. If

you approach persuasion in a dishonest way when trying to get your users to sign up, it will eventually backfire when users find out once they start using your product.[15]

Conclusion

While there are many other ways we can anger our customers, impolite design and dark patterns are the most common culprits. They are loans we take out against our brand equity, or in other words, our trustworthiness. Users do not have infinite patience; just because they don't leave right away doesn't mean they aren't willing to. Although they may need our products and spend a lot of time working through our tricks, the pressure builds, and it only makes for a more violent breakup once they become frustrated enough with the experience that the value they gained is deemed no longer worth it. People do not like to be taken advantage of, plain and simple. They don't feel good when they realize they have been tricked. It's our job to stand up for our users. Take a stand, call out these issues for what they are, and learn how to speak the language of those you work with so you can make your case in a way they will both understand and agree to.

Key Takeaways

1. Emotional harm has a real impact on users, and it can't just be made right by a quick email, phone call, or reply on Twitter from our brand.

2. Politeness serves as a way to establish a positive relationship between everyone involved in a situation and bridges the gap between different backgrounds. This is true not only of face-to-face relationship, but of human–machine interactions too.

3. While most frustrations are caused by ignorance of good design practices, some interfaces are intentionally designed to be complex. We call these *dark patterns*, and they should be avoided at all cost.

---

15 Toxboe, Anders. "Beyond Usability: Designing with Persuasive Patterns." *Smashing Magazine*, October 15, 2015, *http://bit.ly/22ZwRWg*.

4. Dark patterns are used because they work at spiking a single metric, making the designer look good. However, when you look at other metrics, they usually hurt customer retention, customer trust, brand credibility, and likeliness to recommend to a friend.

5. Taking a stand against dark patterns is not always easy. We suggest offering creative alternatives or using persuasive design patterns to achieve better results in an ethical way. If this doesn't work, use the "zoom out" technique. If this is still not sufficient, present counterexamples.

Interview with Garth Braithwaite

The following is an interview with Garth Braithwaite, Senior Experience Designer at Adobe, author at O'Reilly, and Founder of the Open Design Foundation.

1. What, to you, is the purpose of technology?

The primary purpose of technology is to improve life: to improve communication, health, and the general quality of life. To create time by streamlining menial and repetitive tasks so we can focus on greater priorities. To help us identify things we can do to improve ourselves.

2. What role does design play in making the world a better place to live?

Design is the process of studying and improving the way we interact with the world. Good design helps us identify areas where we can improve and leads us to solutions for our problems.

3. Why should designers care about contributing to open source projects?

The majority of the web is powered by free and open source software. It is a foundation for our technology and communication. Designers have a vested interested in pushing the future of the web. Also, the nature of open source licenses provides an opportunity for a diverse group of creators to contribute to this future with relatively low barriers to entry.

4. What contributions have you observed that were the most successful?

The most successful and impressive contributions to open source software have happened when people have found solutions to common problems and released the solution with a free and open license. In these cases contributors are motivated by love of others instead of love of money.

My favorite concrete example is the Nightscout Project (*http://www. nightscout.info*), because of the impact it has on my family. The project is aimed at providing families who have members with type 1 diabetes with constant access to blood sugar levels. Since it is an open source project, parents are setting up the stack themselves and are not required to wait for the government to approve it as a medical treatment. Nightscout's tagline is #wearenotwaiting.

5. How do designers contribute to open source?

Designers contribute to open source the way they contribute to any product; they help identify areas to improve, perform research, and establish workflows to make sure the needs of the people using the product are met.

6. What is Open Design? Why is it important?

The Open Design Foundation (*http://opendesign.foundation*) is a group of designers and developers who realize the great benefits designers could provide to open source software, and in turn, the benefits that designers could realize by participating in software built on love and passion.

Although open source software feels open to developers, it can be intimidating to outsiders. The goal of the Open Design Foundation is to encourage and mentor designers (and anyone else) to contribute to free and open source software.

[4]

Design Can Sadden

There's a wide array of emotions to take into consideration when designing. Most are a lot more subtle than the anger and frustration we discussed in the previous chapter: sadness, self-blame, humiliation, exclusion, sorrow, grief, discomfort, heartache, boredom, etc. Yet, we rarely hear about any of these. Why are anger and frustration often the only emotions being measured by companies? First, the tools and scales generally used to collect information on users' behavior are not appropriate: they don't allow for proper emotional data collection. Second, the best way to understand how people feel is, well, by actually asking them. Unfortunately, this qualitative information is often considered less important and significant than hard quantitative data.

In this chapter, we will explore the different ways we can cause emotional harm to our users by making poor design decisions. Later, we will look at tools to avoid making these errors and to successfully convince all stakeholders in our projects that the emotions felt by our users are important.

The "Dribbblelisation" of Our Users

In the experiences we create, our aim is to delight, to bring joy and value—the goal is always a positive one. That's why designers need to be optimistic to do their jobs. So it's no surprise that we often fail to design for user failure when designing for real users and their very real lives. For examples of this, just take a look at all the concepts on popular websites that showcase designers' work, like Dribbble (*https://dribbble.com*) or Behance (*https://www.behance.net*). We stuff our interfaces with smiling models, epic gateways, giant crisp images of exotic places—all of which will be rare when our app is used by real people. In reality, users' profile pictures may be too far zoomed out or simply blurry, their background images might have low contrast, and their content will be much more subdued than the flashy and idealistic copy we put in our mockups. Often, we launch our products and realize our blunders only when people start using the apps. Even if we keep reminding each other that "You are not the user," sometimes we find ourselves designing neither for us nor for the user, but for some ideal persona that we have in our head. *Someone whose needs and actions magically align with the business goal we have in mind.*

User-centered design (UCD) is effective because it encourages us to really understand the users before designing anything. Only once we know their needs and motivations can we come up with a solution for them. Designing a product and hoping that the users will have needs that correspond to our features just doesn't work. When we really get to know our users, we find that they live very real lives full of ups and downs, of epic adventures and boring afternoons, and of joy and grief. Yet, we often get caught up in our idealistic, positive, and well-intentioned views of what our ideal users might like. Forgetting that our users are not soap opera characters who stop having a life once they are out of our sight is the first mistake a designer can make.

Inadvertent Cruelty

When we forget about the "edge cases," we risk being downright cruel to our users. A poignant example of this was shared by Eric Meyer in his post "Inadvertent Algorithmic Cruelty" (*http://bit.ly/2oa8UhQ*), where he recounted how a well-intentioned feature by Facebook caused him pain. Eric's young daughter, Rebecca, tragically passed away in 2014. At the end of the year, Facebook launched a feature called "Year in Review" in which they cobbled together a review of each user's year with animations and music, using posts and images they had shared. The feature was a big hit and the compilations were being shared by many. But for someone who had had a difficult year, the celebration was turned into a hurtful reminder of that pain. That day, when Eric logged in, he was presented with a large picture of his now deceased daughter, surrounded by dancing figures and balloons (see Figure 4-1). To add insult to injury, the feature didn't allow users to opt out, so he had to endure seeing this over and over again, every time he visited Facebook.

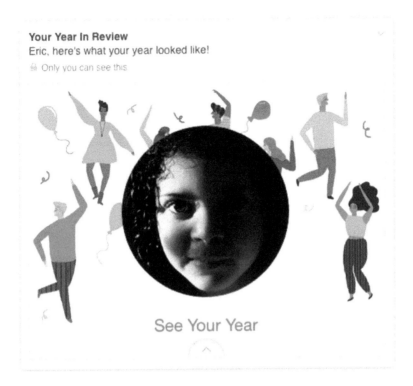

Your Year In Review
Eric, here's what your year looked like!

Only you can see this

See Your Year

FIGURE 4-1.
Eric Meyer's 2014 Year in Review on Facebook, insensitively presenting a picture of his now deceased daughter surrounded by balloons and dancing people (image courtesy of Eric Meyer)

"I didn't go looking for grief this afternoon, but it found me anyway," Eric wrote in his blog post. Unfortunately, he isn't the only one that had to live this situation. Others also had painful memories forced upon them, without their consent. Homes that had burned down, painful breakups, deceased friends… all unfortunate events presented as "highlights." Obviously, no one is deliberately trying to be cruel at Facebook. This feature worked really well for the vast majority of users who had had a great year, the events of which they wanted to be reminded of.

Designers love to surprise and delight their users. We do this by using quirky copy, adding Easter eggs, implementing small features that save a click, or adding details to personalize an interaction. Most of the time, this is a really great practice. However, when we implement a feature meant to celebrate, present a memory, remind of a date, guess a need, etc., *we have to make sure that the user can opt out of it.* Sometimes, seemingly benign elements of the interface can quickly make someone sad.

Another good practice when using user-generated content is to take advantage of all the information available to determine if it's sensitive or not. For example, Facebook could have used a picture's comments to determine if it represented a sad memory. If words like "sad," "sorry," "RIP," or similar were found in the comments, the image could have been excluded from the Year in Review to avoid becoming a trigger of negative memories.

Instant Sadness Triggers

Here's testimony from Chloe Tetreault, a UX designer from Montréal, that shares how Facebook caused her sadness.

July 31, 2013

My dad died at 4 a.m. on July 31, 2013. He was 57. He'd been diagnosed with stage 4 cancer that had spread throughout multiple parts of his body. His illness progressed rapidly from that point, and only three weeks later he passed away.

As ubiquitous as it is, death and the grieving process are an abstract concept to many of us, and even something we actively try to avoid considering wherever possible. We are all aware of the five stages of grief that we're expected to traverse; however, in reality, these grieving phases are experienced differently from one person to the next. At first, I was really emotional and had to externalize and talk about his death with those around me as much as I could—it would help me process things. Yet, as the months passed, my grief became more internalized and I didn't want to talk about it as much with others, feeling that they couldn't understand, or maybe that I could no longer truly express what I was going through. In reality, it's never really over; it just changes, or lightens over time or is spread out, and sometimes, when you least expect it, something hits you back. It's hard to explain.

A few hours after my dad's death, my Aunt France posted an old family photo to Facebook: my sister and I, smiling and laughing with my Dad. It's a nice photo, a good memory. At the time, I remember thinking that it was a thoughtful gesture. People commented and gave their support from there. (I even commented on the photo three days later.)

July 31, 2015

Two years later, I woke up on a Friday morning feeling pretty good; I was looking forward to the coming weekend. I woke up around 7:30, same as usual. Grabbed my phone and started reading my Facebook feed. Then, suddenly, my mood changed. Facebook had resurfaced my dad's picture, posted two years earlier by my aunt. In less than a second, memories of him and his last weeks filled my brain and tears started running down my face. Just like that, in a moment's glimpse of a photo, Facebook made me relive the most painful time of my life without my say, without any way of knowing.

What could I do? Untag myself, maybe, but then the photo would be lost in my aunt's photo collection. It would be hard to find it when I do feel like looking at it.

I mentioned the grieving process as never really being over. Facebook pushing that notification felt like going three steps back into the grieving process. It was horrible. But how could they know? How could they avoid this? I understand that I might want to share some memories, but there are others that I'd rather not share and, even more, I don't want to be reminded of. I didn't need to be reminded of his death; that date is pretty engraved in my memories, forever.

Father's Day, 2016

No matter how many years pass by, there are certain times, like holidays, where it's just difficult, no matter how long it has been. Christmas, his birthday, and Father's Day are the hardest for me. This year again, Facebook reminded me about Father's Day. I dismissed the message. I'm pretty sure I dismissed it last year, and yet got another reminder this year.

It's a really tricky situation, because when Mother's Day comes around, I am pretty happy to get the message.

July 31, 2016

I started writing this story for Cynthia and Jonathan's book at the end of July, perfect timing. On the 31st, Facebook pushed the memory again (since I had never dismissed it). This year, it was a bit easier to see it. Perhaps because I was expecting it more than in the previous years.

Self-Blame and Humiliation

At the most basic level, a user's frustration with our products can cause harm through self-blame and humiliation. They believe that their difficulty to use our products is due to their own failures or shortcomings. Oftentimes we don't realize that these small wounds we inflict on our users can add up over time and cause real harm. The result of this self-blame is people who avoid technology or have anxiety using it in front of others.

Because users are often alone in a task, they don't have anyone to compare their progress to and assume that since the product is used by many people, they must be the only ones having an issue. This can also lead to exclusion, as users remove themselves from using technology to avoid the pain or embarrassment of not knowing how to use it. Users prefer to isolate themselves from what is causing them pain, discomfort, and frustration.

"Power User" Features

There are many strategies to help people who are new to your product and make them feel like they belong. First, don't prioritize "power user" features above those that benefit the "newbie." These features are great, but should never come at the cost of an onboarding feature.

SHORTCUTS

Be wary of options accessible only through shortcuts and actions represented only by an icon (and no text). Think about how you are going to make these actions discoverable. While a tool tip is very useful, it only works with a cursor (not on mobile phones and tablets). One great solution is the search feature under the "Help" menu in many macOS applications (see Figure 4-2). Instead of simply presenting the search results that match the input, it teaches the user where they can find that feature the next time they are looking for it. Note that the menus also show the shortcuts next to every item, which is also a good practice to help new users. We do wish that they would spell out the Alt key (or Option key) shortcut completely, though, instead of using the ⌥, ⇧, and ˆ symbols, which systematically take more time to read and are not always printed on keyboards. Google Docs does a better job at this (see Figure 4-3).

FIGURE 4-2.
macOS offers a great search feature under the Help menu of many applications: instead of just showing the results, it automatically shows where the option can be found in the menus.

Format	Tools	Table	Add-ons	Hel
B Bold			⌘B	
I Italic			⌘I	
U̲ Underline			⌘U	
S̶ Strike-through		Option+Shift+5		
x² Superscript			⌘.	
x₂ Subscript			⌘,	

FIGURE 4-3.
Google Docs spells out the shortcut, using the word "Option" instead of ⌥

MAKE THE SETTINGS ARE UNDERSTANDABLE

Every time you add a new setting, ask yourself if the added complexity is worth it. If you must keep every single setting option, consider hiding and grouping complex and unnecessary options together. Make sure you give great explanations of what these options are. Even better, add visual examples directly in the setting pages. Your users, even the "ninja" ones, will thank you for it. We often tend to overestimate the capacities of our users to understand and know every detail of our products.

Often, we simply ignore these users and allow them to leave because we don't think they can be helped without a lot of resources. We tell ourselves that we design for "power users," "modern users," or even "a younger demographic." The truth is, anyone can have issues, and we are leaving money on the table by not designing products that are easy enough for everyone to use.

The Options That No One Understands

Cynthia tells us about the time she gave a workshop to a group of game designers.

I was recently giving a workshop at a big video game company. I asked the crowd who considered themselves "hardcore gamers," and the vast majority said they were. To give you an idea, every time I showed a screenshot in my presentation, they had to identify what game it was from, before I named it. They knew *all* the games, even the obscure, indie ones.

Later in my presentation, I showed some gameplay options from the very popular video game Diablo 3 (see Figure 4-4) and asked them what "vertical sync" and "clutter density" meant. The room went dead silent. I'd always assumed that I wasn't enough of a hardcore gamer (power user) to know exactly what these options were. But here I was, in front of a group of game developers and level designers—people who, I assumed, knew these things really well—and yet they couldn't explain what these options referred to specifically. Why are these options visible to all of the gamers? Doesn't this contribute to making new players feel excluded? Couldn't these advanced settings be grouped together? Should they have an added explanation, or even better, some examples, to help with discoverability?

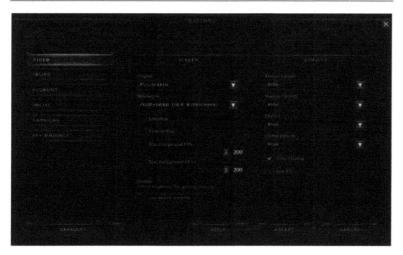

FIGURE 4-4.
Diablo video options. The menu has some options that not many people (even "power users") understand, let alone can explain.

Allowing for Abuse

Another way we can cause emotional harm to our users is by forgetting to design safeguards to prevent abuse. Initially, designers were responsible for a very small portion of the product. Over time, they have taken on an increasing amount of responsibilities, crafting the whole user experience, the interactions, and the visual design, and often taking part in product decisions as well. With this shift comes added responsibility. If we get stuck with a narrow vision of what the product should do, we neglect all the potential uses people might have for our products—uses that we have not planned for and that don't fit any of our personas.

Personas are great tools to ensure everyone in the company can put a face on their users, but they can bite us back when they are representing a limited spectrum of our users. One persona that we systematically forget to design for is the bad one. The popular saying "There are no bad users, just bad designs" is simply untrue. We are not talking about users who aren't comfortable with computers, but the nefarious ones. By designing for all people, we must accept that there are aspects of humanity that are reprehensible. Hate, bigotry, bullying, racism, and malice can all be found in users. Especially in social products, where users interact with each other.

For example, if an app allows users to send files around the internet, there will always be users who want to abuse it to send spam, or for phishing, or to send something nasty to a person they despise. It's surprising how products can be abused. We need to be mindful of the harsh reality that *users can act badly*. It is our responsibility to design for this and protect the people using our products.

How do we design to prevent abuse? Designing to mitigate abuse is never intuitive. This is the same reason why technology security is never perfect. Our job is to think about this when we design our products. Here are some good questions to get us most of the way there. They should be asked when designing any new or enhanced feature:

- How might people abuse this feature to hurt others?
- If this feature is being used for abuse, how can a user take action against it?
- Is the banning system top down or bottom up? If it's top down, can it scale?
- What are the consequences of someone abusing others? What do they have to lose?
- If we add more safeguards, do they distract or discourage interaction from the rest of the users? If so, is there a way to do so without distraction?
- Are there any incentives for someone to abuse?

Never hide behind the very easy excuse, "I just put the tool online; what people do with it, I can't control." Twitter's founder used to say that it was "a communication utility, not a mediator of content."[1] However, this has led to the platform becoming a paradise for racists, trolls, and harassers. The problem is so bad that Dick Costolo, Twitter's CEO from 2010 to 2015, wrote:

---

1   Schiffman, Betsy. "Twitterer Takes on Twitter Harassment Policy." *Wired*, May 22, 2008, *https://www.wired.com/2008/05/tweeter-takes-o/*.

We suck at dealing with abuse and trolls on the platform and we've sucked at it for years. It's no secret and the rest of the world talks about it every day. We lose core user after core user by not addressing simple trolling issues that they face every day.

I'm frankly ashamed of how poorly we've dealt with this issue during my tenure as CEO. It's absurd. There's no excuse for it.[2]

With social products, the abuse can be clear or it can be muddied. Sometimes it's just not clear that abuse is occurring versus what might simply be a bad argument. For example: "Ugh, I hope you die." Is that worth a ban? It is certainly abrasive, but depending on the context, perhaps not worth a consequence. On a video game chat, wishing for your opponent's death is very common. The same sentence in a direct message on a social network is not only harsh but illegal.

A social network might deem such behavior okay until there is a history of it. Others might ban users altogether when they see anything like this. Social products have to decide where they will draw the line and how they deal with the gray areas. Facebook and Twitter have both made strides in improving how they deal with abuse, such as making reporting easier or providing a way to mute others, but at the time of this writing, they have taken a weak stance against the gray areas and in many cases even against clear-cut abuses.

How to Prevent Causing Sadness

We know that no designer or engineer at Facebook is ill-intentioned when creating new features. Once again, blaming a single person would not be helpful. But good intentions aren't enough to excuse us from causing harm through the products we design. Let's instead look at what could be done to prevent creating instant-sadness moments.

AVOID CONFUSING A CHANGE OF EMOTION WITH A CHANGE OF STATE IN A DATABASE

For a computer, a reaction on Facebook is literally a number in a column. We can have a hypothesis as to why a user might "like" something, but we shouldn't associate the word used on the button to the

---

2   Warzel, Charlie. "'A Honeypot for Assholes': Inside Twitter's 10-Year Failure to Stop Harassment." BuzzFeed News, August 11, 2016, *http://bzfd.it/2lHtmHl*.

actual user's emotional state. For example, before Facebook introduced the newer reactions (love, haha, angry, wow, and sad), the only ways someone could interact with someone else's content were either through a comment or a "like." We would witness situations where someone with a very sad status update would have a bunch of people pressing the "like" button on that update. They obviously weren't happy about their friend's unhappiness. Pressing the "like" button was a way to show empathy. It meant something along the lines of "I've read your update," "I'm with you," or "I like to see that you are expressing your emotions." There is a major difference between pressing the "like" button and actually liking something.

Also, if you are using an algorithm to build a feature, make sure it uses the right data, not an icon as a proxy of an actual emotion. Users understand that when something has "likes," it doesn't necessarily mean it's actually *liked*. Unfortunately, algorithms aren't always designed to know the difference between an empathetic "like" and a genuine "like."

DON'T UNDERESTIMATE THE POWER OF SYMBOLS

That leads us to a second important point: be very careful with the words and symbols used to interact with content. They should always accurately represent the action that the user is doing. For example, Apple Mail used to ask its users to press a "thumbs down" button to move an email to the junk folder (recently, this icon was changed to an inbox with an "x"). It seems logical, then, to press a "thumbs up" button (associated with the action of liking something) when the user wants to remove an email from the junk folder, moving it back to the inbox (see Figure 4-5). This works in theory, but in practice, not all emails that are safe (not junk) are liked. Here's an example that happened to us: a credit card statement from a new financial institution was wrongfully classed as junk by Apple Mail. We then had to "like" that email in order to send it back to the inbox. Trust us, *we most certainly do not like our credit card statements, but the software forces us to say that we do.*

FIGURE 4-5.
Apple Mail asks the user to "like" an email in order to move it from the junk folder to the inbox

You may be thinking, "It's just a symbol, how harmful can it be?" Well actually, symbols linked to actions are pretty powerful! All these smileys, thumbs, likes, stars, and hearts can carry a great load of emotion.

When Airbnb, the online service that enables people to list or rent properties, changed its rating system from stars to hearts, it saw a massive increase in conversions. As reported in an article on Co.Design, while a star is "a generic web shorthand" that doesn't carry a lot of weight, a heart is "aspirational" and creates an emotional response:

> For a couple years, registered Airbnb users have been able to star the properties they browse, and save them to a list. But Gebbia's team wondered whether just a few tweaks here and there could change engagement, so they changed that star to a heart. [...] To their surprise, engagement went up by a whopping 30%. "It showed us the

potential for something bigger," Gebbia tells Co.Design. And in particular, it made them think about the subtle limitations of having a search-based service.[3]

Hearts and stars are not the only symbols carrying a lot of emotional weight. Smileys are equally, if not more, powerful. Research has shown that *the human brain* no longer knows the difference between emoticons *and emotions*.[4] You did not misread that: our brains no longer distinguish a smiley face from an actual smiling face!

A team of researchers has demonstrated that the brain is now processing emoticons with the same signals that were previously only there when processing real emotions on human faces. They showed 20 participants the smiley symbol, :), along with real faces and strings of symbols that don't look like anything, and recorded the signal in the region of the brain that is activated when we see faces. While the signal was recorded at a higher level when looking at real faces, it was surprisingly higher when people saw the emoticon.[5]

REMEMBER THAT EVERY USER WILL DIE

This is certainly not the sexiest part of designing for a service, but if your company plans on staying in business for a long time, it will inevitably be confronted with the death of some of its users. Have you planned for the cancellation of your service when someone dies? How will you handle the situation for a grieving person trying to access their loved one's account? What paperwork will you require to make this transition as painless as possible, while remaining secure? Are you going to send emails (or worse, physical mail)?

Some companies handle the situation in a very sensible way. The microblogging platform Twitter is a great example. When someone wants to request the removal of an account, they are directed to a form where every detail has been carefully designed (see Figure 4-6). The

---

3 Kuang, Cliff. "How Airbnb Evolved to Focus on Social Rather than Searches." Co.Design, October 2, 2012, *http://bit.ly/2nitrgS*.

4 Eveleth, Rose. "Your Brain Now Processes a Smiley Face as a Real Smile." Smithsonian. com, February 12, 2014, *http://bit.ly/2mpa3kG*.

5 Churches, Owen, Mike Nicholls, Myra Thiessen, Mark Kohler, and Hannah Keage. "Emoticons in Mind: An Event-Related Potential Study." *Social Neuroscience* 9:2 (2014): 196–202.

form uses down-to-earth wording, and sensible options. First, the section about the deceased user is neutrally titled "Report details." This is a sensible choice of wording to avoid referring to the deceased person directly—we can only imagine that the person filling in this form doesn't need a large-type reminder that their loved one is dead. Also, there is an "Additional information" field, but it is clearly indicated that it is optional. This allows the user to give as many or as few details as they feel comfortable with. Finally, Twitter needs to know the relationship between the applicant and the deceased user. Instead of asking for a detailed explanation, they minimize the impact of the question by leaving only three choices: family member or legal guardian, legal representative, or other. Note also how verbs are completely absent from the questions. We can assume that this process is hard enough; being forced to state that you *were* the deceased's mother would be a useless and painful reminder.

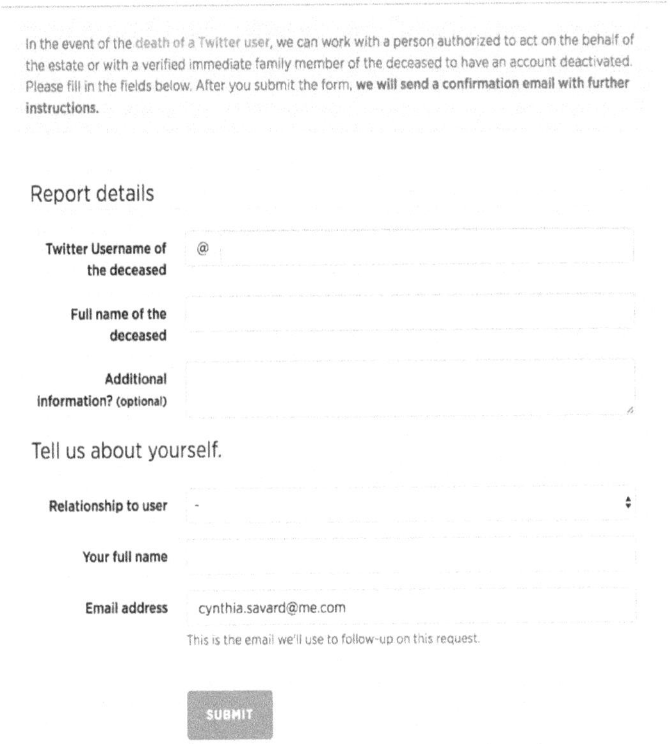

In the event of the death of a Twitter user, we can work with a person authorized to act on the behalf of the estate or with a verified immediate family member of the deceased to have an account deactivated. Please fill in the fields below. After you submit the form, we will send a confirmation email with further instructions.

Report details

Twitter Username of the deceased	@
Full name of the deceased	
Additional Information? (optional)	

Tell us about yourself.

Relationship to user	-
Your full name	
Email address	cynthia.savard@me.com

This is the email we'll use to follow-up on this request.

SUBMIT

FIGURE 4-6.
Request form on Twitter's website to deactivate a deceased user's account (source: *https://support.twitter.com/forms/privacy*)

USE THE SAD SHERIFF

If you work within a team, designate a person that will act as the Sad Sheriff for a week. This person has the following responsibilities:

- Advocate for the unhappy user in every meeting they attend.
- Review all of the current designs with that unhappy mindset.
- At the end of the week, share their findings through a collaborative journal (this can be a simple Google doc that is shared with everyone and written as a list of bullet points).

For example, in a brainstorming session, the Sheriff would systematically be the one reminding the team that not everyone is having a good day. They might say things like "Someone grieving and canceling the account for their partner might find the copywriting of this email really rough," or "Someone visiting our website looking for help might have difficulty finding the information they need."

Then, you can define a rotating schedule of Sheriff types. For example, week one is the *Grieving Sheriff*, week two is the *Sick Sheriff*, week three is the *Sad Sheriff*, week four is the *Depressed Sheriff*, week five is the *Disabled Sheriff*, etc. Also, every team member should be in the rotation, not only designers. No one should be designated for more than a week (or sprint, if that is your choice of development methodology), because let's face it, it's hard to always be the party pooper.

REPRIORITIZE FEATURE DEVELOPMENT

Developing a new product can be costly. Companies, even large ones, don't have endless resources to spend. Therefore, our features generally get prioritized in a table with two axes: frequency of use and percentage of users affected. What most people use, most of the time will be implemented first (see Figure 4-7).

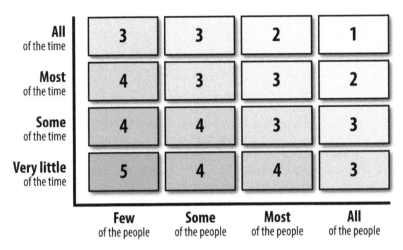

	Few of the people	Some of the people	Most of the people	All of the people
All of the time	3	3	2	1
Most of the time	4	3	3	2
Some of the time	4	4	3	3
Very little of the time	5	4	4	3

FIGURE 4-7.
Typical feature prioritization table

This method works really well, except that it makes it virtually impossible to include safeguards against rare but potentially tragic situations in the roadmap. If when we ask ourselves "What's the worst that could happen?" there is a chance that something might hurt or kill someone, then it should become a priority, even if the odds of this happening are really slim. The safeguards put in place can be annoying to some users. However, we argue that it's perfectly acceptable to be annoying to most of your users, if it's to avoid causing pain to a minority. *Preventing harm to a user should always triumph over a feature.* For example, when a visitor searches for "sad," the blogging platform Tumblr will offer help instead of actually showing the search results (see Figure 4-8). Even though this might be useless to most people and forces an extra click, it could make a great difference for a few users. It is absolutely worth it. In addition, it shows other users the genuine care Tumblr has for them and the rest of the user base.

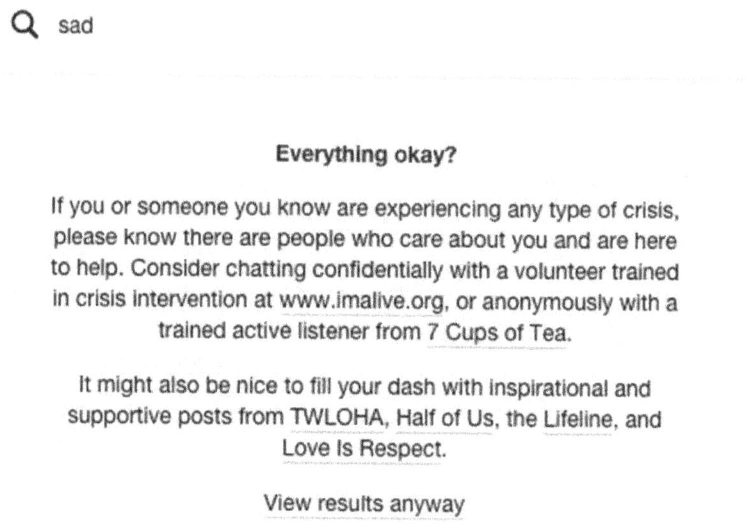

Q sad

Everything okay?

If you or someone you know are experiencing any type of crisis,
please know there are people who care about you and are here
to help. Consider chatting confidentially with a volunteer trained
in crisis intervention at www.imalive.org, or anonymously with a
trained active listener from 7 Cups of Tea.

It might also be nice to fill your dash with inspirational and
supportive posts from TWLOHA, Half of Us, the Lifeline, and
Love Is Respect.

View results anyway

FIGURE 4-8.
Screenshot from Tumblr.com. A search for "sad" offers help instead of
presenting the results.

ORGANIZE CATASTROPHIC BRAINSTORMS

We are well aware that the quantity of potential individual situations
makes it impossible to design for every single scenario. To uncover a
lot of them, there's a very fun 45-minute activity that can be done as a
group. We call this the *catastrophic brainstorm*. The goal is to invite as
many people as possible into a room and ask them, "What's the worst
that could happen with our new feature?" Each participant has to come
up with a catastrophic scenario, write it on a Post-it, and stick it on the
wall. Encourage all participants to be creative! We find that coming up
with funny examples at the beginning helps to break the ice. Once you
have a bunch of Post-its on the wall, vote for "the worst thing that could
happen." The top three scenarios should then be seriously considered
as a priority on the roadmap.

CHANGE YOUR USUAL TESTING SCENARIOS

When performing user tests, we always start with a script that sounds like "Hi! Welcome! Take your time, you can't make a mistake, if you can't complete a task it's because of our design, don't blame yourself!" And so on. We go above and beyond to make sure the testers are comfortable, monitoring the temperature of the room, making sure they don't feel observed, offering them their favorite coffee, and being extra reassuring as soon as they struggle. While all these efforts in making the participants comfortable are commendable, they certainly contribute to getting optimal results from relaxed participants. In real life, our users aren't always in a perfectly designed environment, using the latest equipment, in an ideally lit room, with all the time of the world in front of them.

Raising the stress level

What if we were to raise the stress factor a little bit, by asking participants to complete a task with a time limit? We're not suggesting that we transform all test sessions into highly stressful events, but maybe one of the five tasks that have to be tested could be done under slightly more stressful conditions. You could try to incentivize testers with sentences like "If you finish in less than four minutes, we will donate $5 to this charity," or "Try to make less than three wrong clicks to find the information," or even "We will time you doing this task to see how long it takes." The results will greatly differ: they will better reflect reality and help uncover some edge cases. (Also, if a user can't find information on your website when they are a little bit stressed, then you know improvements are required!)

Performing usability testing in context

The majority of usability tests take place in conference rooms, laboratories, or even hotel meeting rooms. This is convenient for observing people interacting with the product in a controlled environment and removing distractions and interruptions, while restraining the amount of variables. However, depending on the expected usage scenario, it might be appropriate to test in a realistic environment, with all the expected distractions and imperfections. Before making this call, visit the location as an observer. Note the different issues that could come up during testing and take many pictures.

Considerations for on-location user testing include the following:

- Do you have the physical room to observe without causing further distraction? Can you be in the same physical space as the testers without having to move equipment?

- Are there any safety concerns?

- Are there potential confidentiality issues?

- Will the technological setup meet your requirements? Is it reliable?

- How about the lighting and noise levels? Can you actually hear and see your testers? This is especially relevant if you have observers in a different room or plan to record the testing session.

While we would like to say that every test should be performed in the actual environment where a product will be used, we understand that it is not always possible. However, it is possible to reproduce certain distractions and suboptimal environment setups in a laboratory. For example, instead of testing in an airport, one could record the sounds from a terminal and play the soundtrack during the test. Consider making props, having actors around, etc. Keep in mind that in most cases, testing with actual users and with realistic use cases is more important than testing in the actual environment.

DESIGN FOR FAILURE

Harm is often caused not by design, but because designers forgot a specific use case. No product is perfect: there are always bugs, incomplete pages, elements that are forgotten, or simply errors caused by external factors. Therefore, it's crucial that the failures are taken into consideration. At the very least, every product should have a strategy for the following situations. What happens when:

- There's no cellphone data?

- The app, or software, crashes?

- The device crashes?

- There is no GPS reception?

- The service is down?

If you're designing a website, make sure that the 404 error page is clear and useful. It's also a great opportunity to be creative. Think of the empty states of your product, not only when the users are onboarding, but also if they erase all the data. Make sure that you always have clear error messages that not only explain the problem, but also offer suggestions for the next steps. In addition, the tone we take in our error messages should not make the users feel they are to blame or that the errors are their fault. Instead, these messages should convey our empathy and take responsibility. The chat app Slack is a good example of using clear error messages with indications of the next steps required (see Figure 4-9).

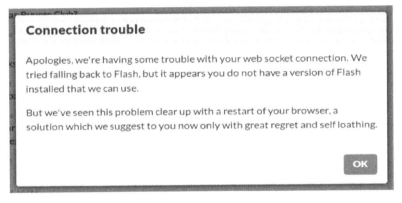

FIGURE 4-9.
Screenshot from Slack. The "connection trouble" error message is a great example of using copywriting to display information about what went wrong, how to fix it, and a little empathy that shows there are humans behind the software.

The Importance of Error States

Serena Ngay, a designer from Ottawa, Canada, tells us how she was hurt by technology recently.

I recently had a personal encounter with cruelty in design...

March 27, 2015. A typical Friday turned into one of the worst moments in my life. During a lunch meeting, I received a phone call from my dad. He sounded scared. My sister, who had been battling cancer for years, was now in critical condition and the doctors said there was nothing more they could do. My sister was dying in a hospital in Toronto, and I didn't know how many hours or minutes I had left to see her.

The distance from Ottawa to Toronto is 450 km (280 miles). That's an estimated time of 4.5 hours by car.

As we were on the highway, I received a call from my sister. She was on FaceTime calling her friends and family, saying her goodbyes. My sister's very last words to me were delivered through FaceTime. That thought alone blows my mind. I am grateful that technology has evolved so that I was able to have those critical moments through this small device in my pocket. But I also now know how cruel technology can be.

Our phone call was cut short, and these error messages kept popping up...

I remember when FaceTime launched, there was a commercial showing a happy friend calling another happy friend. What would that scenario look like if stress and emotions were running high?

Picture this: we are four hours away from Toronto in a rented car racing down the 401 highway, my mom is in the back seat crying with an anxious dog beside her, and I'm in the passenger seat fumbling with my stupid phone trying to figure out what this error message means. It's not clear what the issue is and I have no idea how to fix it.

"Not available for FaceTime"? What does that mean? Is there a connection issue? Do I have to change my settings? ... Did she die?

It was in that moment I realized: *this* is design (see Figure 4-10).

I am positive that the designers of FaceTime never imagined this user scenario. But the reality is that the designers that worked on FaceTime aren't any different than us.

FIGURE 4-10.
This FaceTime error message doesn't tell the user what the next steps are

Conclusion

"What if?" should be asked over and over again. What if the user had a terrible year? What if the event someone is organizing using our service is a sad one? What if the group created using our tool is in memoriam? What if the seemingly ridiculous product ordered on our website holds a very high emotional value to some customers? It is hard for us to think this way—we like to imagine how we might delight our users, but people appreciate more than just delight. People appreciate kindness, respect, honesty, and politeness as well.

Emotional harm is something we often overlook because it is hidden. Now that you are aware, make sure to call it out when you see it! The majority of the harm described in this book isn't purposefully considered and committed; it happens without a thought to these consequences. Raising these issues might just be enough to turn your company's decisions away from emotional harm and toward respecting users' emotions. It will, at the least, start an important conversation at your place of work. Users might not always get to speak, but you can stand up and speak for them.

Key Takeaways

1. User-centered design (UCD) is effective because it encourages us to study, research, and really understand the users before designing anything. Only once we know their needs and motivations can we come up with a product for them. Designing a product and then hoping that the users will have needs that correspond to our features just doesn't work, and quite frankly is counterproductive.

2. When we create a feature meant to celebrate, present a memory, remind of a date, guess a need, etc., we have to make sure that the users can opt out of it. By not doing so, we might force a hurtful reminder on our users.

3. Avoid confusing a change of emotion with a change of state in a database. We shouldn't associate the word used on the button to the actual user's emotional state. Don't underestimate the power of symbols linked to actions. These smileys, thumbs, likes, stars, and hearts carry a great load of emotion.

4. To avoid causing sadness, implement a "Sad Sheriff" in your team, organize catastrophic brainstorming sessions, always think of error states, and consider changing your usual user test setup to reproduce stress scenarios.

Interview with Maya Benari

The following is an interview with Maya Benari, Designer and Web Developer at 18F, and former fellow with Code for America.

1. How do you see bad design affecting citizens?

Bad design hurts us all. When something is designed so poorly that you can't complete the task, that is a problem.

Imagine a veteran coming back from war, trying to use their GI Bill to find a college they can afford, but they can't understand how to navigate complex websites to find the right school.

Imagine your family member is sick in another country, and you can't get through the passport renewal process to see them in time.

Imagine the thousands of people trying to escape poverty in the US, struggling to complete confusing paperwork to get the help they need.

What these all have in common is how they make you feel: disempowered, frustrated, and helpless. The system that was supposed to help you stands in your way. It feels like a betrayal.

2. How are you and your team contributing to help solve it?

18F (*https://18f.gsa.gov*) is a civic consultancy for the government, inside the government, enabling agencies to rapidly deploy tools and services that are easy to use, cost efficient, and reusable. We are transforming government from the inside out, creating cultural change by working with teams inside agencies who want to create great services for the public.

We are a trusted partner for agencies working to transform how they manage and deliver services to the public.

We do this by:

- Putting the needs of the public first
- Being design-centric, agile, open, and data-driven
- Deploying tools and services early and often

The government, bound by centuries of history and pressures to comply with outdated laws, has historically built online experiences which reflect the bureaucracy rather than human needs. Democratic values reinvented for the 21st century mean accessible, responsive, representative, simple, and effective services. Simplicity is key, both in the interface design and the content design. Plain language and good UX enable users to understand the content or service the first time they read or use it.

The American people should influence digital services, which should in turn influence government policies. Here's a recent example: President Obama proposed a ranking system for universities. Research showed us that people didn't just need rankings, they wanted facts and figures. 18F and the US Digital Service (USDS) built a website with the Department of Education to show data like how much graduates make after 10 years and how well people are paying off student loans for any college or university. Being user-focused changed what was built in spite of the initial policy recommendations.

3. How did you find your way to designing for government?

Prior to designing at 18F, I completed a year-long fellowship at Code for America, working with the City of San Antonio to harness the power of technology to help solve community problems. Before that, I practiced design and web development for startups, design studios, nonprofits, and the entertainment and medical industries. Designing for the public good was the only thing that felt worthwhile to me.

4. How do you think design will be able to improve the interaction people have with their government?

Good civic design, at its core, is about access. Access to government services and information must be available to all, regardless of circumstance, device, or location. Good design ensures this. It means that people can get the right help, sooner, with less stress.

I remember this from Jennifer Pahlka's talk at the 2015 Code for America Summit: "The barriers that matter here are not technical. You have an amazing team of people who understand policy, law, and regulation and are some of the best in the country. *Your organizational structure is not set up to understand what users experience when they are using your service.*" (Emphasis added.)

Design can improve the interaction people have with their government by having clear and open communication with the public. By understanding what people experience when they use public services, we can design and build better systems to meet the public's needs.

5. How can designers help make government better?

Designers can help make government better by speaking out and by raising voices of those not commonly heard. Designers should include people from a range of backgrounds, races, locations, gender identities, income levels, ages, and levels of experience into the design process. From initial user research interviews to testing prototypes, government services should be built for, with, and by the American people.

One way to do this is by making partners inside and outside of the places they work. There is no knight in shining armor coming to save the day. We're all here to work on hard problems together.

Directly, designers can apply to work in the government, in our Digital Coalition of 18F, USDS, agency digital service teams, and the Presidential Innovation Fellowship. There are opportunities to contribute from short to longer term. Designers in the private sector can contribute to our work on GitHub (*https://github.com/18F*). We're committed to making everything we work on open from day one.

6. How can the layperson help improve design in the government?

Sometimes it's just about starting a conversation. If you're interested in helping, you can:

- Share feedback
- Take surveys
- Participate in user research
- Tweet at us @18F
- Write about experiences you had using government services
- File an issue on GitHub

We all have a contribution to make. Our unique skills, talents, and perspectives are what make this country great and are needed to help solve some of the hardest problems this generation faces. Let's work on this together.

7. What does it take to design in government?

Designing in government is not so different from any other industry. To be successful, you need empathy, patience, and flexibility. There are absolutely more restrictions around our designs, since by law we are required to do things that may be considered "icing on the cake" in the private sector. For example, for accessibility we must ensure there is good color contrast or that every element on a page can be accessed with a keyboard. Thus, there are certainly key concerns when it comes to empathy, patience, and flexibility.

To design in government, you need empathy:

- Empathy toward government employees. Many government employees face resistance to change. They are driven to serve the public, but have potentially faced years of people telling them they can't do things to serve the public better or backlash for trying something new. They are doing the best they can and have a wealth of domain knowledge that can help serve the public better.

- Empathy toward the structures. Bureaucratic structures were set up to protect the American people. You wouldn't want the US government to play games with your Social Security number. However, these structures can hinder effective technology from being built unless you work to understand the intention behind them. Understanding and staying aligned with the goals of the bureaucracy allows you to suggest new approaches when appropriate.

- Empathy toward the public that are using government services. You don't know who's on the other end of a service. They could be someone who's feeling stressed out or relaxed, using high-speed internet or a rural cellular connection, who speaks English fluently or as a second or third language. It's important to build for all spectrums of people.

To design in government, you need patience: things often move slower in government, so you need patience and steadfastness to see things through. Working in government can be hard, but it's also incredibly rewarding.

To design in government, you need flexibility: a willingness to try new approaches, make partnerships with people you wouldn't expect, or whip up a quick prototype can speak a thousand words.

8. How do you avoid designing something that will cause harm?

You can avoid designing something that will cause harm by:

- Being aware that we all have biases and working against those

- Keeping up on web and accessibility standards

- Interviewing people across a range of ages, races, locations, interests, abilities, and gender orientations

9. What is the purpose of technology to you?

Technology is a tool. It's like this big lever that can accelerate and connect people, places, and things. Technology is an enabler, something that creates an even playing field. There's a darker side of technology because it can also reinforce biases. Every tool has the imprint of its builder in it, so every tool has certain assumptions baked in. It's always important to ask yourself: What are these assumptions? How is this tool shaping outcomes?

For example: Am I assuming everyone has a large smartphone with blazing fast internet connections because that's what's in my pocket? Or instead, are they on an inexpensive phone going through subways with limited connections and a limited amount of data because that's what they can afford?

You should never rely on technology solely. Rather than decide if a service is effective by looking at analytics, observe how people are using it in person. Rather than spend months and millions of taxpayer dollars building out a new digital tool, perhaps all you need is to provide a better diagram.

10. What role does design have in making the world a better place to live?

Design is about solving problems. The word "design" comes from Latin *de signare*, or "to mark out." We can take ideas and put them into physical form or action. By thinking up new ideas to solve old problems, we can reinvent the world we live in.

We can build sandwich rating apps or work on improving people's lives—it's up to us to choose. When we shift our focus toward service, purpose, and solving the problems of humanity, design can help make the world a better place. Designers are saving the world by translating, communicating, simplifying, and helping people achieve their goals.

As designers, we can take an active role in society by asking these questions:

- What does it mean to be an engaged citizen?
- What problems is the world facing that I can help with?
- What did I do to contribute and make the world better?

If we see our country going in a direction that we're not okay with, we're responsible for that.

[5]

Design Can Exclude

IN INNOVATING CONTINUOUSLY AND making our technologies more powerful, we risk making them more complex and more expensive. Unfortunately, this results in excluding a lot of people from them. As we said before, design is a bridge into technology, and it's up to us to define how practicable this bridge will be. We do this by making sure we follow these rules:

- It is *accessible* by everyone.

- Everyone feels *welcome* and *safe* to cross it.

- Its access is *just*.

Designing a technology that doesn't follow these three rules will cause hurt in a very different manner from that described in the previous chapters. If a group of people are unable to cross the bridge, then they are excluded: they get left behind socially, politically, economically, and creatively. They miss out on all the things technology can enable for them.

In this chapter, we will look at how bad design can exclude people from these three angles: accessibility, diversity or inclusion, and justice. We will give best practices and tangible arguments to build a case in your company or to a client. We will learn from examples where design played a central role in creating an unjust situation and come up with ways we can help. As with all the examples in this book, we look at these design mistakes with a critical perspective in order to learn from them, not to blame the organizations, companies, or designers behind these decisions.

Intuitive Design to Access Technology

Jonathan tells us a personal story about his in-laws.

I will never forget the moment I truly understood the power that design held over people and how many people out there are just waiting for good design in order to access technology. I was visiting my in-laws one weekend and my father-in-law asked me for some help with his computer. It was a somewhat dated desktop computer running Windows XP. As I reacquainted myself with the OS, he sat next to me at attention with a pen and notepaper. All he wanted was to do a few simple things: watch videos on YouTube with closed captions on, listen to the radio, and learn about science and history, his favorite subjects. After a few minutes explaining to him where to find the internet browser, where to type in the URL, and how to search, I let him take over the mouse and keyboard. I reviewed his notes and I was shocked at how many steps he had written for what I thought were simple tasks. He even had notes about how to turn on the computer, log in, and move the mouse around. I looked over to see how he was doing, and he was struggling. He kept apologizing. He didn't need to apologize. Here was a man who grew up in a fishing town in Iran and had never had access to a computer until very recently. His wife, who was more comfortable with computers, came over and was able to help him by explaining it in Farsi, his native language.

When I got home, I decided to buy them a nice new laptop with the friendly-looking Metro user interface from Microsoft. I thought they would have a much easier time with a computer that was faster and, so I thought, more user-friendly and modern. When it arrived, they were so excited. We all crowded around and fired it up. The excitement soon went flat as we struggled through the setup. I showed them around the "cards" and how to pin apps. When I returned a few weeks later the laptop was off in the corner, not being used. They said it was too confusing. I felt I had failed them, failed to give them access to the wealth of benefits that technology has to offer. Instead, they felt more alienated than ever. My father-in-law politely told me not to bother and blamed himself.

A week or so later their phone contracts ended and we decided to get them iPhones, but that day I was too busy to show them how to use the phones. We simply set up accounts for them on iCloud and had to run out the door. When we visited them the very next week, I was dumbfounded. There was my father-in-law, watching YouTube, and with captions! He also showed me the Persian radio app he had found. The two of them had downloaded a slew of apps in Farsi. I hadn't spent a second teaching them but there they were, exploring on their own. If that wasn't enough, my 97-year-old grandma was in town soon after, and after dinner she surprised me by bringing out her iPad! She showed me how she loved playing games, reading books, looking at pictures of family, and watching videos in her own language.

That was it, I was sold. I would have never imagined my grandma, a woman born in the late 1920s, before color TV, before radar, heck even before Scotch tape, using an iPad! All it took was for the design and interface to be easy enough to learn. The intuitiveness users find in iOS and touchscreen interfaces allowed these people access to technology and the vast information, innumerable tools, and global connection that come with it. It allowed them to be participants in a part of society that wasn't accessible to them before. Before that moment, they were excluded from technology, left behind while others benefited from it.

Accessibility

Inclusive design, design for all, digital inclusion, universal usability, and similar efforts address a broad range of issues in making technology available to and usable by all people whatever their abilities, age, economic situation, education, geographic location, language, etc. Accessibility focuses on people with disabilities—people with auditory, cognitive, neurological, physical, speech, and visual impairments.

—W3C WEB ACCESSIBILITY INITIATIVE (*HTTPS://WWW. W3.ORG/WAI/USERS***)**

Although accessibility best practices have been established for years, very few websites meet even the lowest conformance standards of the Web Content Accessibility Guidelines (WCAG). These guidelines were developed by the World Wide Web Consortium (W3C), an international community that works for developing web standards. There are three conformance levels: A (the lowest), AA, and AAA (the highest).

People with disabilities are considered as an afterthought by many companies because they (mistakenly) think that this group represents a small subset of their customer base. Therefore, they are often excluded from the benefits of technology. Companies, especially small ones like startups, think that they don't have the resources to do the extra work required to accommodate all users. This is a persistent myth that can cause a company not only to exclude those with disabilities, but also to miss out on a slew of high-value benefits associated with meeting their needs.

A CASE FOR ACCESSIBLE DESIGN

Before we dive into accessibility considerations for designers, let's look at why we should make our services accessible and who will benefit.

It affects a lot of people

Let's take a look at some numbers on the prevalence of disability, to help you build a case. To start, according to a US Census Bureau report, "About *56.7 million people—19% of the population*—had a disability in 2010, according to a broad definition of disability, with more than half of them reporting the disability was severe."[1] (Note that these are American statistics and that someone can have multiple disabilities. Also, these numbers are self-reported, which means they could be under the actual statistics.)

While these numbers vary immensely from one reference to another, we can all agree that the prevalence is much higher than what we would guess from looking around. The reason is simple: people don't walk around showing off their disabilities. Moreover, people with disabilities often are isolated by poorly designed services, environments, and workspaces.

Here is a more detailed view of the prevalence of different disabilities that affect how people interact with our designs:

Visual impairment

> Approximately 4% of the American population aged 12 and older have a self-reported visual impairment (visual acuity of 20/50 or worse), according to the Vision Health Initiative (*http://www.cdc. gov/visionhealth/data/national.htm*).

---

1   United States Census Bureau. "Nearly 1 in 5 People Have a Disability in the U.S., Census Bureau Reports." Census.gov, July 25, 2012, *http://bit.ly/1yfsJ2k.*

Color blindness

An additional 4.25% (approximately 8% of males and 0.5% of females) of the population is color blind in some way or another, whether it is one color, a color combination, or another mutation (*https://nei.nih.gov/health/color_blindness/facts_about*).

Hearing impairment

Approximately 13% of Americans aged 12 and older have hearing loss in both ears (*https://www.nidcd.nih.gov/health/statistics/quick-statistics-hearing*).

Literacy

Approximately 12% of American adults cannot read; i.e., have a "below basic" proficiency level (*https://nces.ed.gov/programs/digest/d15/tables/dt15_507.10.asp*).

Other physical and cognitive disabilities

Adding to the numbers above, we must consider all the users that have other physical, neurological, or cognitive limitations, including 19.9 million people that have difficulty lifting and grasping, 15.5 million adults that struggle with daily activities (such as cooking, using the phone, etc.), and 2.4 million people that have Alzheimer's, senility, or dementia (*http://bit.ly/1yfsJ2k*).

It is good for business

Looking at the numbers above, it's clear that if your company doesn't follow accessibility guidelines, it is potentially excluding a lot of potential customers. If more people can access your service, your potential market increases.

While talking with people from the blind community, we learned that it's common that once they find a service or a website that works well for them, they will stick to it and be very loyal. Accessible websites are great for customer retention.

And your business will benefit in another way from accessibility measures. Making the content accessible to screen readers makes it readable by search engines' "spiders," the software that crawls websites to populate the search results. In short, this is really good for your search engine optimization (SEO). And if your SEO is really good, you won't have to spend as much on ads (AdWords) to appear in the first results when users search for your keywords.

It benefits everyone

If it's good for people with disabilities, it can benefit everyone, in one way or another. A great example is the sidewalk ramp. While it is designed specifically for people in wheelchairs, it is useful to parents pushing a stroller. It also helps older people that have difficulty climbing stairs. It's useful to anyone walking a bike, pushing a grocery cart, or pulling a child's sled in winter (yes, this is common in snowy cities). This is just one of many examples of a feature that might be necessary for a small portion of the population but ends up benefiting almost everyone at one point or another.

On the web, accessibility measures benefit people without disabilities in many situations, such as people using a slow internet connection, people with temporary disabilities such as a broken arm, and people with changing abilities due to aging.

It's required by law

This is pretty straightforward: making your website accessible is required by law in many countries.

It's simply the right thing to do

The argument for accessibility reminds us of the "green" movement. While it can be a great business move to recycle, sometimes it's just about not being a jerk to the environment.

We can go very far to convince everyone that it makes sense to invest in accessibility. But maybe we shouldn't even have to build a case. Even if it didn't make sense from a business perspective, *it's simply the right thing to do.*

MAKING YOUR SERVICE ACCESSIBLE

Making a website accessible can be a simple process. It depends on the type of content (text, images, animations, videos, etc.), the size and complexity of the site, and the tools used to build the site. If your site relies heavily on external services and widgets, it might be difficult to make it entirely accessible. Many accessibility features are easily implemented if they are planned from the beginning of development and design, and there are already a lot of resources that can help developers meet accessibility standards. Here, we want to focus on what designers can (and should) do.

Don't rely on color to convey information

The first easy thing to consider is color. Never rely on color as the sole way to differentiate items. Instead, use colors to complement what is already visible. Use of color is extremely common in navigation menus, to highlight the selected item. In this case, it's very easy to simply make the text bold, italic, or underlined to represent that it is active or in a different state from the other elements in the same list. Also, we often come across financial data presented in red when negative, with no other indications that the number is below zero. This is highly problematic for people who suffer from deuteranopia (red–green color blindness). Dashboards with graphs are frequently problematic too. Using textures in addition to colors for bar charts will fix the problem. As for line graphs, use different weights or styles (dotted, dashed, etc.) in addition to colors (see Figure 5-1).

 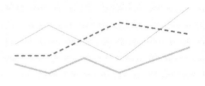

Same weight but different colors is not accessible   Different weight, style and color is accessible

FIGURE 5-1.
Comparison of accessibility in charts. On the left, an example of a typical line chart using only colors as a differentiator. On the right, adding a dashed style and a different weight makes this perfectly legible for people that are color blind.

A good example of an accessibility feature can be found in the very popular color-association game TwoDots: the designers included a setting that adds shapes to the colored dots (*http://bit.ly/2mKo9y1*). We argue that not only does it look nice (see Figure 5-2), but it helps even those without disabilities!

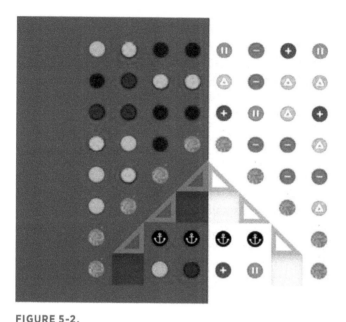

FIGURE 5-2.

The app Dots. Accessible mode is shown on the right. Not only does it look really good, but it's also helpful for everyone.

Pick high-contrast text colors

Consider "background versus foreground" color contrast. When using colors for text, they must offer a certain contrast ratio with the background. This number is higher depending on the level of WCAG conformance (*http://bit.ly/2nQnrNW*). We suggest using tools to help calculate your website's contrast ratio. One very simple and useful tool is the Color Contrast Check, built by Jonathan Snook, a Canadian web developer who advocates for accessibility (*http://bit.ly/2nUkk95*). We often hear designers complaining that their creativity is limited by color contrast ratio. They think that there aren't enough possibilities of high-contrast colors to meet the standards. While these do limit the possibilities, there are still a massive amount of color combinations to pick from. Also, you can always suggest increasing the type size: this will allow for a less contrasting color combination, while still meeting the standards. We really like the website Colorsafe (*http://colorsafe.co*), which offers many accessible color palette options (see Figure 5-3).

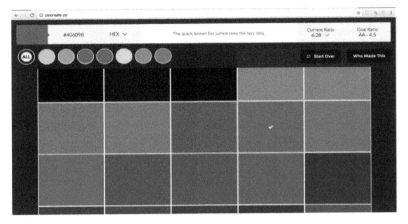

FIGURE 5-3.
Colorsafe.co suggests color palettes that are accessible on different background colors

Color selection is only a small section of the accessibility guidelines. The next steps to take are dependent on the content types.

Use alt text

For every image on your website, make sure you include alternative (alt) text. Complex images should have more extensive descriptions near the image, such as a caption or a descriptive summary in a surrounding paragraph. The alt text is important for users who have visual impairments and rely on screen readers to access the web. They won't "see" the image; they will "hear" its description instead. Images that are purely decorative don't need alt text. However, make sure the alt text is very descriptive when necessary, which is most of the time. For example, an ecommerce website that has three pictures of the same t-shirt should have different alt text for every image, mentioning what is seen exactly in the images. This could look like this: "man wearing a green t-shirt," "green t-shirt folded in a drawer," and "green t-shirt seen from the back." Do not write only the name of the product presented in the photo, as the user might lose important information conveyed by the imagery. In this example, it's obviously a male t-shirt based on the description of the first image, something a blind person could miss if the alt text only referred to "a green t-shirt."

Avoid text embedded in images

Another bad idea is to put text directly in the image. While this is no longer popular with calls to action on buttons, we still often see it on banners (or hero images). If you really have to do this, perhaps because the platform doesn't allow you to superimpose text on your image, make sure the alt text is always updated with the current content. This is especially important because these large banners tend to promote special offers, and you definitely don't want anyone to miss this information!

Provide context for hyperlinks

Always provide context for hyperlinks. This means that links like "click here," "more," or "continue" should be avoided. Instead of "For train schedule click here," write this: "Consult the train schedule." Make sure the hyperlink is understandable by itself.

Simplify your textual content

Reduce the amount of text, avoid unnecessary adverbs, and make your sentences shorter. As discussed previously, the literacy level in America is surprisingly low. In addition to people with low literacy, many users are navigating the web in their second (or third) language. More words won't make you look more intelligent to them; it will make you less understood. The Hemingway Editor (*http://www.hemingwayapp.com*) is a great tool to test the grade level required to understand your content. To be as inclusive as possible, aim for grade five and lower. Another great resource is the Plain Language Action and Information Network (PLAIN) website (*http://www.plainlanguage.gov/site/about.cfm*). They advocate for the use of plain language in government communication, but their tips and guidelines are valuable for anyone.

Avoid automatic image sliders (or carousels)

Carousels should not be used on a website. First, low-literacy users don't have time to read the content before it disappears. Second, they are difficult to navigate for users that depend on screen readers. To quote the famous researcher Jakob Nielsen, "Auto-forwarding carousels and accordions annoy users and reduce visibility."[2] If you have to deal with a website that already has an image slider, make sure the user can at least pause it. Also, add large controls: the tiny dots at the bottom of the slides are not sufficient to control it. Many tests have shown that not only do carousels underperform (*https://erikrunyon.com/2013/07/ carousel-interaction-stats/*), but people interact very little with them. Users tend to simply ignore them because they look so much like ads. Replacing them with static content will likely do a favor to your company and your users.

Design accessible forms

Forms are an inherent part of the web. They are used to log in, to create accounts, to communicate, to complete purchases, and for many other reasons. Some designers try to come up with new designs all the time. While originality is usually a great thing in graphic design, we argue that forms are an exception to the rule. They tend to perform better when they are standard. As with many elements in this list, *everyone* benefits from a well-organized and highly usable form. To make sure your form is accessible, look for the following considerations, in addition to the other design guidelines:

- Keep the labels visible when the user is filling in the fields. Don't put labels inside the fields unless they remain visible when focused (see Figure 5-4).

- Don't use gray placeholders inside the field (either to replace the field or as a hint on the required format) if unnecessary. They are not always read by screen readers and create more errors than anything.[3]

- Make sure the form can be filled using only the keyboard and the Tab key.

- Group all error messages at the top of the page, and repeat them next to the erroneous form control. Make sure there is a textual explanation of the error; don't just highlight the field in red.

---

2 Nielsen, Jakob. "Auto-Forwarding Carousels and Accordions Annoy Users and Reduce Visibility." Nielsen Norman Group, January 19, 2013, *https://www.nngroup.com/articles/ auto-forwarding/*.

3 Sherwin, Katie. "Placeholders in Form Fields Are Harmful." Nielsen Norman Group, May 11, 2014, *https://www.nngroup.com/articles/form-design-placeholders/*.

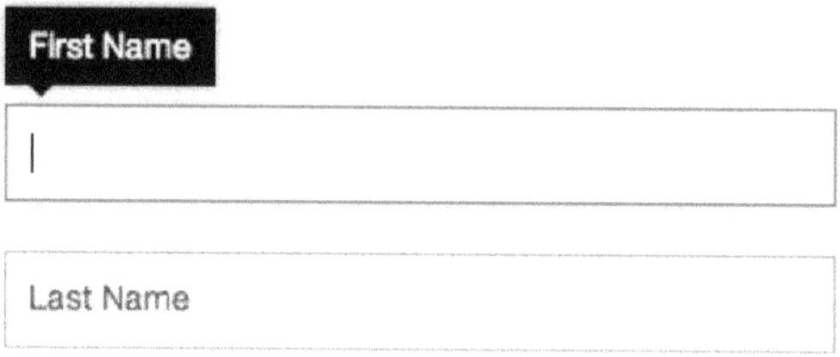

FIGURE 5-4.
An example of an in-field label that remains visible when the field is selected
(source: *http://konigi.com/blog/making-infield-form-labels-suck-less/*)

There are many more guidelines, but we decided to highlight a few that are easy to start with. In addition to these, every designer should read the W3C accessibility guidelines (*https://www.w3.org/TR/UNDERSTANDING-WCAG20/*). It's a simple read that will turn into a great investment of your time.

Consider accessibility outside of the browser

Disabilities don't only affect people when they are browsing the web. Designers from all industries should learn about accessibility. Think of the lack of consideration for left-handed people in product design. Even though left-handed people make up 10% of the population, product designers often exclude them. Peelers, rulers, scissors, notebooks, tin openers, corkscrews, and even knives are difficult to operate by lefties! Print design also has shortcomings. The readability of signage in public spaces is often deficient, and the use of colors as the sole differentiator is very common. Can you imagine how confusing a metro map with colored lines is for someone that is color blind? What about the consequences of relying only on colors for traffic lights? A friend who is color blind recently told us that he always assumed that having a "green light" was a metaphor, since he sees the traffic lights as white, yellow, and red. Some cities have traffic lights that use different shapes for green, yellow, and red lights (see Figure 5-5). The Canadian Association of Registered Graphic Designers (RGD) has published a free handbook (*https://www.rgd.ca/database/files/library/RGD_AccessAbility_Handbook.pdf*) that summarizes best practices for signage and print design. Check it out, it's insightful.

FIGURE 5-5.
Traffic lights in Halifax, Canada. In Canada, most traffic lights have special shapes to assist people that are color blind. (Source: *http://bit.ly/2oIH5kB*.)

Treat internet access as a human right

We rely on technology in every aspect of our lives: work, education, government services, recreation, shopping, and health, to name only a few. We should design for an accessible web to ensure social inclusion. The actor Christopher Reeve, who became paralyzed after a spinal cord injury, once said (*http://webaim.org/articles/motor*):

> Yes. [The Internet is] an essential tool. And, literally, a lifeline for many disabled people. I have Dragon Dictate. And while I was in rehab, I learned to operate it by voice. And I have enjoyed corresponding with friends and strangers with that system. Many disabled people have to spend long hours alone. Voice-activated computers are a means of communication that can prevent a sense of isolation.

Internet access has been declared a human right by the United Nations (*http://bit.ly/2n5fmrj*). The Internet, with a capital I, is now a public domain, and its construction is as important as the planning of the cities we live in. The same way that we wouldn't (or at least shouldn't) design a city that is not accessible to people with physical disabilities, we shouldn't create a web that only a selected group can visit. In architecture, when a place restricts its access to a certain caste of society, it is called *hostile architecture*. Let's work together to avoid building a hostile web.

INSPIRING CHANGE WITHIN YOUR ORGANIZATION

To gain allies within your company, try organizing regular accessibility demonstrations. You could, for example, invite someone from the blind community to give a demonstration of their use of your product. If you do so, make sure you offer fair compensation for their time. Invite them back a month or two later to see how your product has evolved. It can be very awkward to watch someone fail at navigating your website, but this painful feeling is necessary to build proper awareness and empathy.

Another way to rally your colleagues to the cause is by teaching everyone to use screen readers. Try making everyone use a screen reader for an hour, either on their computers of their phones. This turns out to be a challenging (and fun!) activity that can be done in pairs.

As a designer, you have the power, and duty, to inspire change. Making your product or service accessible will turn out not only to be better for your organization but also to ensure no one is excluded from the benefits of technologies. Web accessibility is essential to create equal opportunities. When websites, tools, apps, operating systems, and software are inclusive and accessible, they empower everyone to socialize, to be independent, and to benefit from what most of us take for granted. When they are not, they are harmful by contributing to reinforcing inequalities and excluding a diverse group.

Diversity, Inclusive Design, Design for All

While accessibility focuses on people with disabilities, inclusive design (or universal design) addresses a broad range of issues in making technologies available to and usable by all people, whatever their abilities, age, economic situation, education, geographic location, gender, language, etc. These concepts are closely related and should be considered together.

"Designing for all" means something very different from one company to another. It's important to take a moment to understand who is included in your "all." For example, to a blogging platform, "people without WiFi access" might not be a significant segment to design for. But for a video game company, they represent a very important group of users that have specific requirements. In the same vein, designing for "people with slow internet connections" isn't very important for a financial software company that develops a product intended to be used offline. But for any product used online, it's significant.

Inclusive design should take into consideration all *current* users and all *potential* users. *In the US, up to 13% of the population has yet to use the internet.*[4] This number is as high as 48% in China, and reaches 90% in some countries (*http://bit.ly/2oFKZbn*). It is estimated that there are up to 4 billion people worldwide that have yet to come online. Any company that designs with them in mind will be better positioned to survive in the long term. Think about people with slow or spotty internet connections, and people who are using the web in their non-native language, accessing it through different devices, etc.

WORDS, POWERFUL WORDS

The most common and subtle way we exclude others is through our words. Our unconscious bias bleeds through and we don't even know the walls we are putting up when we use one word instead of another. A simple pronoun, which for some wouldn't get a second glance, can alienate others and stop them from engaging. *Saying who we include doesn't make us more inclusive, it ends up excluding everyone else.* We can make people feel unwelcome in our products by the words we choose. A basic example is if our marketing copy states "He will love it" readers assume the product is for men. If it says "She will love it," readers assume it's for women.

Many sign up forms may make people feel excluded when they ask for gender, or even worse, for the sex. Most offer two options: "male" or "female." For many people, that doesn't represent their biology or identity and they feel excluded by it. The question can also bring doubts about the intention behind the question. "Why do they need to know my gender?" one might ask. "Are they collecting my information for their own gain?" and "Will this change my experience in some way?" If we don't need to know the user's gender, we should consider leaving it out completely. Many companies require this information for no other reason than because they've always asked for it. If you are asking

---

4   Anderson, Monica, and Andrew Perrin. "13% of Americans Don't Use the Internet. Who Are They?" Pew Research Center, September 7, 2016, *http://pewrsr.ch/2ciill0*.

because you want to know what pronoun to use to talk to your user, consider simply asking "What is your preferred gender pronoun?" If you really need it for other reasons (statistical, etc.), consider adding a blank option that people can fill if they don't identify to male or female.

At this basic level, this bias can lose customers, hurt people, or create a few angry tweets that are quite bad for public relations. However, when this bias infiltrates entire industries and societies, it becomes destructive. It sends a message to those excluded that "you don't belong here." This can show up in the text we use in our interfaces, marketing websites, and in our communities.

This is something that we fail at more often than we would like to admit. The trouble with bias is that it's very hard to detect in oneself. That is why it helps having a diverse workplace and circle of friends. We need input directly from other perspectives and groups. We need them to call us out on our bias. The more often we get this correction, the better our perspective becomes. This bias also shows itself in the images we choose. If all your promotional and mockup images use a typical nuclear family models (dad, mom, one girl, one boy) it sends a message "this app is for certain types of people" and makes many customers feel excluded.

Once again, gender is not the only factor to account for. In general, it's a good practice to avoid asking unnecessary information. When you must collect information and the reason might not be obvious to everyone, explain how you intend to use the information. Be very careful with the options you give for the answers. One error we often see is under the "how old are you?" question, the options are the following: 18–25, 26–35, 36–45, and 45 +. A 47-year-old will feel like they are considered "old" by this organization, since they don't even get to have their own categories. A much more sensible option would be to add "46–55," "56–65," and "66+." Even if you already know you won't get many respondents in the last three categories, it won't take you much longer to merge them in your results.

DIVERSITY-CONSCIOUS DESIGN: CHALLENGING THE STATUS QUO

You can participate in making diversity conscious design decisions. This means questioning things that seemingly are insignificant and inclusive, and look at them from a different perspective. Here's an example from Sweden:

A group of city officials in Karlskoga, Sweden, noted that after snow-storms, they would first remove the snow from the major streets and then from the sidewalks and bike lanes. Looking at the transport behaviors, they found out that this snow routine benefited men and hurt women. This is because men are more likely to use their cars, while women walk more and use more public transportation.

By prioritizing roads intended for car use, the city also prioritizes accessibility for the mode of transport that men prefer.

This policy design also hurt the "walker" group in a very physical way. In hospitals, the majority of ice-related injuries were happening to women. By inverting the order of the snow removal, they could then make the city more practicable for pedestrians, which in return will encourage more people to take public transport, reducing the traffic, therefore benefiting the driver group too, in the long run. Also, by designing a different route, the city becomes more accessible to everybody, including children and teenagers that can't drive.[5] Urban development and policy planning are areas that should be invested more by designers.

This unfortunate situation happens when we don't question and challenge what has always been done. This is common in the physical product design field. Industrial designers use anthropometric data to make decisions. These tables include all measurement of the human body. For example, it will list the average height, reach, size of the hands, circumference of the wrist, distance between the eyes, etc. Designers then use this information to define the shape, size and position of objects. Unfortunately, some of the very popular databases are compiled from measurements of a military population. This means that there's an overrepresentation of tall, thin, athletic, and young men in these averages. Another issue is that the average male and female bodies today are very different than they were 10 and 20 years ago. We are much taller and bigger than back when the measures were taken.[6]

---

5   "Gender Equal Snow Clearing in Karlskoga." Includegender.org, February 18, 2014, *http:// bit.ly/2oKbHPO.*

6   Roe, R. W. "Occupant Packaging." In *Automotive Ergonomics,* edited by B. Peacock and W. Karwowski. London: Taylor and Francis, 1993. 11–42.

While using anthropometric databases is better than designing at random, it does come at a risk. Car interiors, work environments, tools, and medical supplies are all known to be generally less suitable for women, people of different ethnicity, older generations, and larger people.

In the medical field, research shows that up to 50% of surgical tools have been designed for a male population and are too large and uncomfortable for people with smaller hands.[7] If there is one kind of tool that you wish to be perfectly adapted to the hands using it, it's a surgical tool! A closely related issue is that some medical supplies are designed using Caucasian measures. For example, nose and lip sizes differ between African Americans, Koreans, and Caucasians.[8] This creates a problem with the adjustment of breathing masks that are designed for specific facial features (see Figure 5-6).

We found a third example that is quite disturbing. Some researchers combed through a decade of data on road accidents in the US. They found that females tend to die more and have more injuries in car accidents. The odds of female drivers wearing their seatbelts having a serious injury are 47% higher than their male counterparts! This is because of safety features that are designed with men in mind. The position of the headrest, for example, doesn't offer the best support for a smaller neck.[9]

---

7   "Addressing Women's Needs in Surgical Instrument Design." MDDI, November 1, 2006, http://bit.ly/2lHr6zH.

8   Yokota, M. "Head and Facial Anthropometry of Mixed-Race US Army Male Soldiers for Military Design and Sizing: A Pilot Study." Applied Ergonomics 36 (2005): 379–383.
    Kùu, H., D. Han, Y. Roh, K. Kim, and Y. Park. (2003). "Facial Anthropometric Dimensions of Koreans and Their Associations with Fit of Quarter-Mask Respirators." Industrial Health 41 (2003): 8–18.

9   Bose, Dipan, Maria Segui-Gomez, ScD, and Jeff R. Crandall. "Vulnerability of Female Drivers Involved in Motor Vehicle Crashes: An Analysis of US Population at Risk." American Journal of Public Health 101:12 (December 2011): 2368–2373. doi:10.2105/ AJPH.2011.300275

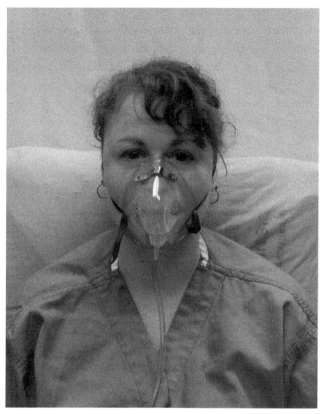

FIGURE 5-6.
This breathing mask is difficult to adjust for people with different nose and lip sizes (photo by James Heilman, MD, *http://bit.ly/2om1lgE*.)

When designing for a different group than yourself, make sure you do so for the right reasons. Design for things that are really different (physically), not for differences that are perceived by society. Dell learned this the hard way when it introduced its laptop marketed toward women called the Della in 2009 (*http://geekfeminism.wikia.com/wiki/ Della_computers*). Women don't need a different physical object than men when it comes to laptop use. Making a laptop pink is *not* an inclusivity measure. The same goes for "female-friendly" cars like the SEAT Mii by *Cosmopolitan* (see Figure 5-7). The issue here is not a car company trying to market to women (finally). The problem is that they do not address the safety features that are not designed for smaller people. They offer the car in purple and announce that it "will handle everything from an impromptu night out, to an afternoon shopping trip. [...]

Whatever you feel like doing, whenever you feel like doing it, the whole car adapts perfectly, on the inside and the outside. It's all up to you..." (*http://bit.ly/2ni4zKq*). Following a much better path, Volvo worked on a car designed by and for women in 2002. While they did come up with solutions regarding storage, they also addressed the car's interior to make it more suitable to women. Here's a description of the features taken from their website (*http://volvocars.us/2oOrGcG*):

> A key ambition in developing the YCC was to ensure that the driver, regardless of height, would be able to sit correctly when driving and have the right line of vision too. The result was Ergovision (patent pending)—ergonomics and optimum line of vision in one system.
>
> Your whole body is scanned at the dealership, then this data is used to define a driving position just for you. This is stored in digital form on your key unit. Once you get into the driver's seat and dock your key on the centre console, the seat, steering wheel, pedals, head restraint and seat belt will all be adjusted automatically to suit your personal build. The result is a sound driving position with the best line of vision for you.
>
> If you want to alter the stored position, you can change the settings of the various car components in the system, then store that set of data on your key unit. The system will warn you if your line of vision is wrong by means of the lenticular hologram, an eye symbol displayed on the A-pillar, between windscreen and door.

This is a much better approach to inclusive design that ends up benefiting everyone.

It's important to note that while none of the examples mentioned here were intentionally designed to do so, they did result in certain groups of people being discriminated against. Such unintentional discrimination happens with many services, systems, policies, tools, and architectural and industrial designs. As designers, we can, and should, participate in these decisions and challenge the status quo.

FIGURE 5-7.
Screenshot from Seat's corporate website (*http://www.seat.co.uk/about-seat/ news-events/corporate/new-seat-mii-by-cosmopolitan.html*). Girls just wanna have fun? We would argue that girls also want to be safe.

Injustice

Justice is a difficult concept to grasp. It involves understanding what is just, a topic which has always been hotly debated and is greatly influenced by cultural and value systems. So let's define justice not as a specific destination or value, but as a *goal or intention for equality, fairness, lawfulness, and morality.* The aim of this section is to give a few examples of how bad design can cause injustice and shed light on the importance of design's role in delivering justice to those who need it.

FOOD STAMPS

In the US, there is a program that helps people with low incomes by providing access to groceries and healthy food. This creates a "safety net" that allows citizens to gain stability and build better lives for themselves and their dependents. It is called the Supplemental Nutrition Assistance Program (SNAP), but often referred as the food stamp program. In 2015, as many as 45.4 million Americans required assistance. They rely on accessing this service to provide food for themselves and their families. Let's take a look at what these people face when seeking help online. When looking for examples of food assistance, we found four bad examples.

Take a look at Figure 5-8. Where should someone go to apply for assistance on Alabama's website (*https://www.myalabama.gov/services*)? Should they click on "Get Assistance" at the top right? Good try, but that would only offer help with the website. Details on the food stamp program can be found under the title "Food and Nutrition Assistance," but when the View button is clicked to view more information, it opens an error pop-up, as if the user had made an error. The site requires the user to be logged in, but there's no place to create an account or log in on this page.

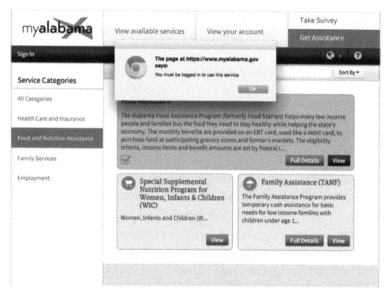

FIGURE 5-8.
Alabama's page for accessing food and nutrition assistance. The website uses an alert to explain that users must be logged in to access some information.

Other states did not do much better. Indiana's website (*http://www.in.gov/fssa*) was down. In Indiana, those seeking aid would have reached a dead end, with no useful information about the next steps except for a recommendation to try again "later" (see Figure 5-9).

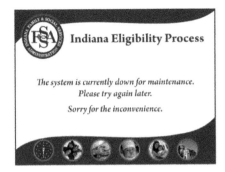

FIGURE 5-9.

Indiana's website was down for maintenance for quite some time

On Iowa's website (*https://secureapp.dhs.state.ia.us/oasis/oasis0100. aspx*), there is very little styling (see Figure 5-10). It gives the impression that it's an error page rather than an official government website. Also, it violates a lot of usability best practices, it has almost zero affordance, and there is no hierarchical organization of the information to help visitors.

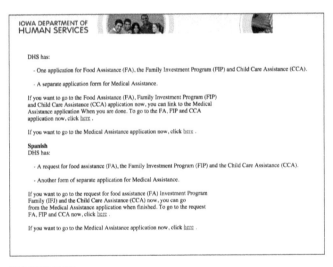

FIGURE 5-10.

Iowa's Food Assistance website—the page looks like an error

Nebraska's site (*http://bit.ly/2n5asuE*) is very hard to decipher (see Figure 5-11). It takes a while to understand that visitors must click the "ENTER in English" link. This website design, like Iowa's, cruelly lacks information hierarchy. Also, the density of text makes it difficult to parse.

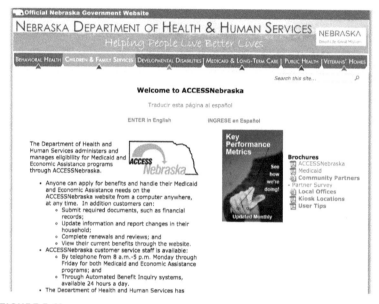

FIGURE 5-11.
Nebraska's food assistance is difficult to navigate

These websites prevent people from getting the services they need. Most of the websites we reviewed required the person to sign up for an account and provide all kinds of information, such as their phone number and address. It's important to note that someone asking for food assistance could possibly not have an address or a phone number to give. Also, the users might have limited access to a computer and the internet, perhaps through a library. They might not have time to go through these extra steps. Lastly, the amount of written information is overwhelming! The illiteracy level in America is surprisingly high, especially within the community requiring assistance.

Here are some statistics provided by the Literacy Project Foundation (*http://literacyprojectfoundation.org/community/statistics*):

- 3 out of 4 people on welfare can't read.
- 20% of Americans read below the level needed to earn a living wage.
- 50% of the unemployed between the ages of 16 and 21 cannot read well enough to be considered functionally literate.
- Between 46% and 51% of American adults have an income well below the poverty level because of their inability to read.

It's painful to imagine someone worried about their food situation, already feeling a bit apprehensive because of the stigma around needing assistance, being deterred by websites like these. These sites should have a higher standard of usability because they provide such critical services. Governments need to spend their resources on designing clear, easy-to-use websites.

PARKING TICKETS

One of the purposes of parking restrictions, aside from the revenue they generate, is to make sure parking is available to everyone. If people were allowed to park in one spot for too long, others wouldn't get a chance to visit that area's stores, businesses, homes, etc. They also exist to ensure traffic fluidity, when the traffic is heavier at a certain point of a day. The reasons, time periods, and laws for parking limitations abound in cities, and many of these limitations overlap. It's no wonder people get confused! Sometimes, multiple layers of legislation are applied. Over the years, they create confusing conditions, requiring people to retain conditional rules in their minds while they try to decipher all of the information. This is where design could play an important role: to let citizens know what the applicable rules are and how to follow them. Unfortunately, this potential hasn't been realized. *Parking signs are often more confusing than the concepts they are trying to convey.* Law-abiding citizens can (and do) get penalized for not being able to understand restrictions they are actively trying to understand.

It is not uncommon for multiple signs to be stacked as pictured in Figure 5-12. People are left to attempt to decode the information and determine if their current and/or future circumstances meet the requirements posted. We all have similar stories: we drove around searching for a parking spot, and when we finally found one, we spent a good minute reading all the signs to make sure it was okay—only to find we'd gotten a ticket when we came back. If someone with a literacy level high enough to read this book up until this point can't understand these signs, now imagine how much trouble they might pose to someone with a fifth-grade reading level, or someone whose first language is not English.

FIGURE 5-12.

Multiple signs with different rules make deciding if parking is allowed difficult (source: *http://www.thetruthaboutcars.com*)

If you require someone to obey a law, in order for the punishment to be just, that law must be properly communicated. It is otherwise unjust to punish those willing to obey the law. Since communication is critical, the importance of design's role is too. Governments that want to communicate with their citizens need good design. When we think of all the restrictions and the way they are put in place in cities, it's easy to suppose that what we currently have is the best we can do. Some designers have tried, quite successfully, to solve these issues (see Figure 5-13), but these solutions have not yet been adopted broadly. One designer, Nikki Sylianteng, took the bull by the horns and suggested a parking sign that uses a schedule metaphor. It shows clearly, with colors and patterns, when parking is allowed, free, restricted, or forbidden. While some argue that the "original" parking sign is built for visibility, Sylianteng's design is aimed at clarity. She created the design in 2010 while living in LA, but it wasn't until 2014 that she started printing the signs and posting them under the confusing signs outside her apartment in Brooklyn. She gathered feedback from citizens by leaving a "comment" section under it. People loved the new design. It's now being piloted in Los Angeles, CA, Brisbane, Australia, and New Haven, CT (*http://toparkornottopark.com/about*). Sylianteng embodies perfectly the famous quote from John F. Kennedy: "Ask not what your country can do for you, ask what you can do for your country." Like Sylianteng, designers shouldn't always wait for their city to commission them to improve something.

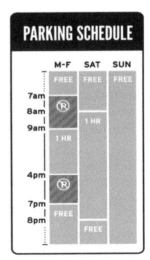

FIGURE 5-13.
A proposed parking sign solution. Nikki Sylianteng, from ToParkOrNotToPark. com, has a simple solution for multiple parking restrictions

PRISON VISITING

Prisons are, obviously, very hard on the families of the prisoners. It can be very difficult to be separated from a loved one, even if they've done something wrong. A family friend of Jonathan's found himself in this predicament. His family was very close and visited him every single week; the only times they would miss a week were if the prison canceled their visit. This would happen without any courtesy call or email notification. The worst part was that the prison was located over 4 hours away. The family would drive all the way there, only to be denied entry and have to drive back. Making the appointment was an obstacle in and of itself. The parents were unable to make appointments due to the website being too confusing. Their daughter was able to eventually figure it out, after much trial and error. We took a look at the website and tried to see if we could understand the problem (see Figure 5-14).

The first thing we see is a giant wall of text, and what seems like a warning or error message. (Not to mention the real warning at the bottom, which confusingly warns you not to use their computing system at the risk of facing prosecution.) They do have Google Translate support, which is a great addition, but the "great" stops there. The giant wall of text is very difficult to understand. It uses terms that people outside the legal system are unlikely to understand and that may cause confusion. In the middle of this giant blob of text we find:

> At no time will any visitor be turned away solely for the inability to make or schedule an appointment. Instructional videos for account activation, forgot password and edit/cancel appointments can be accessed at www.cdcr.ca.gov/visitors.

The URL has to be copied and pasted into the browser's address bar because it's not hyperlinked. It directs the user to a new site where there is a "VPASS account activation" video. When clicked, Google Chrome throws up a warning ("This site is not secure!") and blocks the user from continuing. The user can bypass that warning by clicking on "advance" and proceeding. It then downloads a .wmv file, which, when opened, gives another error (see Figure 5-15).

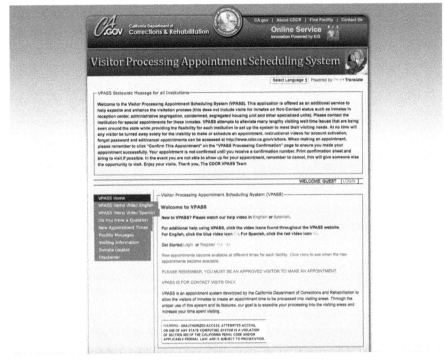

FIGURE 5-14.
Appointment scheduling website for California's prison system (source:
http://visitorreservations.cdcr.ca.gov). The Visitor Processing Appointment
Scheduling System is as complex as its name suggests.

FIGURE 5-15.
Error message in QuickTime. Attempting to view the how-to video ended in an
error.

Families with Apple computers or those that don't have the right
video codec won't be able to figure out how to see their loved ones.
We finally found the one small link on the page that takes you to the
registration process. Once you've registered and logged in, making an
appointment is still daunting. Now, that's a lot of obstacles for anyone

trying to schedule an appointment! Even if they can find someone to help them, it creates undue stress, which they already have enough of. Additionally, encouraging visits is not only important for the inmates and their families, but also benefits society as a whole by reducing recidivism. According to the John Howard Society of Ontario:

> Prisoners who have positive and supportive visits with friends or family members during their time inside are more likely to be successful when they leave prison. This is usually because they have kept the important relationships they need to do well when they're back in the community. Having strong connections with family and community means that people will have a lower chance of re-offending after they leave prison.[10]

THE FATE OF A NATION

(Disclaimer: We are not affiliated with any political party.)

In the 2000 US presidential election, there was a very close race between the two leading party candidates: George W. Bush and Al Gore. The race was neck and neck, with half the voters backing the Republican candidate while the other half were for Al Gore, the Democratic nominee. In the US, each state carries a certain number of electoral votes; voters cast their ballots and the winning party in each state gets those votes (i.e., they vote for people to vote on their behalf). The election had run its course and the votes were being counted. It was an exciting thing to watch. A few states would go to Bush, then a few would go to Gore. It carried on this way until it became clear that the deciding factor would be Florida. Florida was a swing state, meaning that the two major political parties had a similar level of supporters among the voters. The final tally showed just how even that split was. That night, it was announced that Bush had won in Florida by a count of just 1,784 votes. Florida state law required an automatic recount due to the small margin. After a long, drawn-out recount process, the Court's decision came in: in the case of *Bush v. Gore* it was decided that Bush had the victory by an amazingly small margin of just 537 votes out of the 6 million

---

10 John Howard Society of Ontario. "Visiting a Loved One Inside? A Handbook for People Visiting a Prisoner at an Adult Correctional Facility in Ontario." Updated July 2014, available at *http://bit.ly/2n3Qa4h.*

that were cast. After the election, the controversy continued. One of the major contributing factors was the "butterfly" ballot. This is where bad design played a substantial role, and potentially changed the course of the entire nation. In the center are holes for voters to punch through to vote for the corresponding candidate. Take a look at Figure 5-16 and guess which hole you'd have to punch if you wanted to cast your vote for Al Gore.

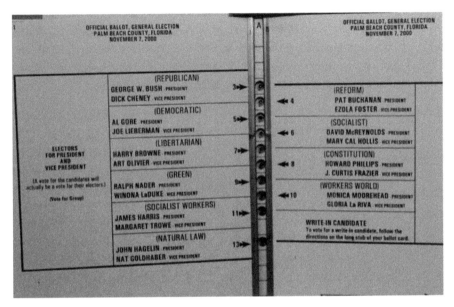

FIGURE 5-16.
The infamous "butterfly" ballot of the 2000 Florida election. Punching the second hole would not give a vote to Al Gore, who is second on the left page, but to Pat Buchanan on the right page.

If you are like us, you chose the second hole and only then saw the arrows. According to the *New York Times*, in Palm Beach County, where the butterfly ballot was used, up to 5,310 people were probably confused by the design and unintentionally voted for Buchanan. The design also confused Bush voters, but only 2,600 voters made that mistake.[11]

---

11 Fessenden, Ford, and John M. Broder. "Examining the Vote: The Overview; Study of Disputed Florida Ballots Finds Justices Did Not Cast the Deciding Vote." The *New York Times*, November 12, 2001, http://nyti.ms/1ng6DJc.

Even if he benefited from this mistake, this is how Buchanan reacted during an interview (*http://bit.ly/2nxnwUR*): "When I took one look at that ballot on election night... it's very easy for me to see how someone could have voted for me in the belief they voted for Al Gore."

Furthermore, an unknown number of voters may have caught their mistake and punched a second time. Many of these ballots were thrown out because of the invalid double vote. The design of the voting ballot was confusing, and even if it caused only one person to miscast their vote, it's prejudicial. It is the right of everyone of voting age in a democratic system to have their say in who should govern them. If it had happened the other way around and the erroneous votes had gone in favor of the Democrats, it would have been an equal injustice.

The design of the butterfly ballot has a few key failures. First, the Gestalt theory of grouping tells us that people perceive grouped items as related.[12] On the butterfly ballot, there are two perceived groups, the left side and the right side. This is why punching in the third hole for the second candidate on the left is very confusing. Furthermore, there should be easy recovery from user errors. Nowhere on the ballot are there instructions on how to use the ballot or what to do should you accidentally select the wrong candidate. The person who designed the ballot was Theresa LePore, a Palm Beach election official. Did she design it absentmindedly? Is she to blame? She actually did design the ballot with her users in mind.

"Being that I'm involved with a federal task force for blind and handicapped voters, I'm particularly sensitive to the special needs of those citizens that fall into those categories," Theresa LePore told ABC News's *Good Morning America* in an exclusive interview. "Palm Beach County has a lot of elderly voters. I was trying to make the ballot so that it would be easier for the voters to read, which is why we went to the two-page, now known as the butterfly ballot."[13]

---

12 Tuck, Michael. "Gestalt Principles Applied in Design." Six Revisions, August 17, 2010, *http://sixrevisions.com/web_design/gestalt-principles-applied-in-design/*.

13 ABC News, "Butterfly Ballot Designer Speaks Out," December 21, 2001, *http://abcn. ws/2nhcR5h*.

Let us recall the old saying: the road to hell is paved with good intentions. LePore had good intentions, she had her users in mind. So where did she go wrong?

"People need to take some responsibility as well for what they do," LePore told the show's host. "Looking back, maybe we should have made it clearer that the presidential candidates were on two pages. I don't know. Again, I can't go back and second guess, because it's something that's done."

She is right that it is almost impossible to know beforehand what will go wrong in a design or how users will perceive what you think is communicated clearly. That is exactly why user testing exists! LePore said she had 25 lawsuits against her, along with many angry letters. The blame, however, is in the broken way these designs are created. The state should have hired a designer who knew how to create a usable design and not relied on an election official. When design isn't valued and made a priority, it fails, just like safety or any other important part of a project that we so quickly rush over when deadlines approach. In this case, that failure had potentially world-changing consequences. If ballot design is a subject of particular interest to you, make sure to visit the Center for Civic Design (*http://civicdesign.org*). They have guides to teach how best to design usable ballots. A lot of the advice is quite basic (use lowercase, avoid centered type, use big type, support navigation with pagination), but other recommendations are not as obvious (avoid political party icons, write at the top how to change a vote). Make sure to stop by the showcases of before-and-after redesigns (see Figure 5-17).

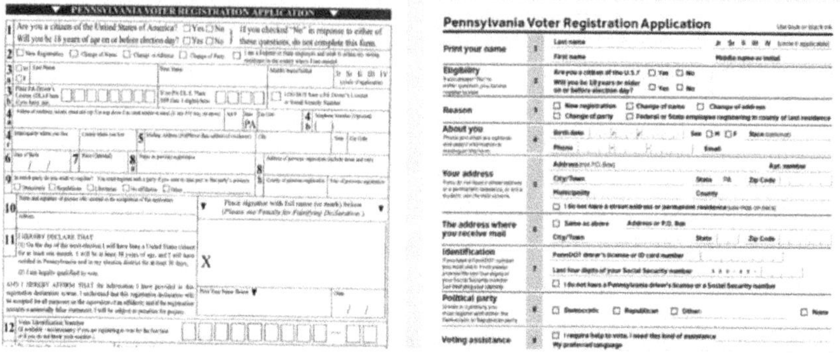

FIGURE 5-17.
Example of a voter registration form before (left) and after (right) the redesign, using the Center for Civic Design's best practices

When design gets in the way of something just, it causes injustice. Our role as designers is to design interfaces that are invisible; to remove any obstacles between the user and the product or outcome we are designing for. Design plays a big role in many important areas of our lives. We rely on good design for communicating and delivering these critical services. We take for granted the role of design, but when it fails it becomes all too clear. We must recognize design's critical role and value in our lives and provide the adequate resources and proper design processes to ensure it *doesn't* fail.

Conclusion

As designers, it is our job to care for the user's interaction with our products. If anything prevents the audience from using it, we have failed and must find the solution. If your ecommerce site wasn't designed for people on mobile devices, that would be a high-priority problem. So it is when we exclude people through all our design choices. When we choose to ignore accessibility or when we forget who our audience is and alienate them, we are not contributing to building the largest bridge, to use the metaphor again. Exclusion is a failure of design. Good design listens to its users; bad design ignores them. Good design goes the extra mile to make sure everyone is happy; bad design takes the shortest path to meet business goals. Good design assumes the designer's point of view is biased; bad design assumes it represents all users. Lastly, we shouldn't wait until we or someone close to us needs it to start caring about accessibility.

Key Takeaways

1. Design is a bridge into technology, and it's up to us how wide that bridge will be. If a group of people is excluded, they get left behind in many ways: socially, economically, and creatively.

2. Making accessibility a priority in your company not only will benefit users with disabilities, but is also a great business decision.

3. The most common way we exclude others is through our use of words. Our unconscious bias bleeds through, and we don't even know the walls we are putting up when we use one word instead of another.

4. Injustice can occur when a rule is conveyed through confusing design (such as parking signs). In these cases, law-abiding citizens can (and do) get penalized for not being able to understand something they are actively trying to understand.

5. Injustice can also happen when information is not accessible to the people in need. It can be available but not accessible; for example, when a website is too difficult to navigate, or when the language used is too complex.

6. The illiteracy level in America (and elsewhere in the world) is surprisingly high, especially within the community in most need of assistance. These people, who need our attention, are oftentimes invisible to the designer.

7. When they notice something that doesn't work, designers shouldn't always wait to be commissioned to improve it. To quote John F. Kennedy: "Ask not what your country can do for you, ask what you can do for your country."

Interview with Dean Hamack

The following is an interview with Dean Hamack, Accessibility Expert at Microsoft.

1. How have you seen bad accessibility design cause exclusion?

I've seen it in a number of ways, but one of the most common errors is when a developer fails to provide text alternatives for visual elements. For example: sighted people take for granted that a text box with a magnifying glass icon in it is a search field. But a blind person using a screen reader has no way of knowing what it is without a proper label. Another example would be providing video content without a text transcript for the hearing impaired.

2. How are you and your team contributing to help solve it?

One of the things we're working on is building a library of accessible web components, which will become the standard for all developers within the company. We're also working on putting together an accessibility blog which we plan to make available to the public. We're not only committed to improving the accessibility of our own products, but also educating outside developers on how they can be part of the solution, rather than part of the problem.

3. How did you find your way to becoming an accessibility expert?

About 10 years ago, I woke up with blurry vision in my right eye. I went to the doctor, and discovered that I had a detached retina. The prognosis was not good, and I was told to be prepared for the complete loss of vision in that eye within 24 hours. Thankfully, one of the best eye surgeons in the country was available, and she was able to restore 90% of it. But that experience really made me think: What would happen if I suddenly went blind? How would I make a living? So I started studying accessibility, and it became a passion of mine.

4. Why is accessibility important?

Accessibility allows people to be independent, and that benefits everyone. When technology can be used to help others overcome limitations, it allows them to excel. And sometimes our greatest innovations come from people who have faced and transcended those limitations.

5. What would you like designers to know about designing for accessibility?

90% of the battle can be won simply by using good semantic markup. Use lists, headings, and paragraphs where appropriate. Use *<a>* tags or buttons for elements that trigger actions, rather than divs or spans. One thing I always say to developers is if you remove all your CSS, your web page should look like a well-formatted, well-structured Word document. If things are confusing or out of order, then it's probably not very accessible.

6. What would you say to those who are worried about spending their limited project resources on accessibility?

First of all, there seems to be a misconception that making websites accessible requires significantly more work, and that's simply not the case. If you follow best practices, it's generally just a matter of adding a few ARIA attributes. Secondly, not providing accessible content can cost you a lot more in the long run—both in terms of lost customers and in lawsuits, such as the one filed against Target in 2006 (which cost them $6 million).

7. What is the biggest challenge when designing for accessibility?

The biggest challenge is building complex UIs like calendars and charts. Basically, anything that requires the user to "see" an element in context, without actually seeing it. The other challenge is educating coworkers and clients on the importance of accessibility, so everyone is on the same team.

8. What is the purpose of technology and design to you?

Some designers see technological advancement as an end unto itself, but for me it always has to be seen as a means toward the end of equipping others. When we set out to design something, the first question we need to ask ourselves is not "How can I make this thing look cool?" but rather, "How can I make it easier for people to achieve their goals?" It doesn't matter if those goals are education, facilitating communication, or simply entertainment.

9. What can designers add to their process to avoid causing exclusion through bad accessibility?

To me, accessibility isn't just about making sites easy for people with disabilities to use, it's about making them easy for everyone to use. The best way to do that is to come at it from the user's perspective, and get their input during the planning stages. And accessibility testing needs to be seen as a mandatory part of the QA process. At Microsoft, sites don't get released until my team signs off on them.

[6]

Tools and Techniques

WHILE WE HAVE BEEN trying to convince you that, as a designer, you have great power and thus great responsibilities (thanks again, Ben!), we understand that we are preaching to the converted. Now, you need to convince the other people on your team: product managers, engineers, the marketing team, and the finance department. We recommend that you perform user tests. They will most likely uncover all the potential issues that could result from your work. There are multiple test possibilities, some more time-consuming than others. There's nothing like user testing in context, with real customers, to teach us about the impact of our decisions when we are designing products; yet we have all been confronted with tight deadlines and inflexible budgets that prevent us from performing formal testing sessions with actual users. At other times, testing, while super valuable, is just not enough to uncover all potential user scenarios. Finally, even the best findings need to be presented in a compelling way, or they will be completely overlooked.

In this chapter we will suggest techniques to prevent a design from causing harm unintentionally. We hope this can help you justify the importance of empathy in your company. Some tools can be used right away, while others require resources or a team. Applying all these techniques won't make your design bulletproof, but it will contribute to reducing the potential harm it could cause.

Gather as Much Data as You Can

One of the simplest ways to convince people of the importance of investing in good design practices is to use insights that come from different data points. A good method to gather this data is to survey internal experts. Customer support representatives should be the first stop on your list. Think of customer support as the "always on, but too late" user research at the company.

They have a very difficult job: they talk to the customer when the product experience has failed. They have to answer for designs decisions they didn't make, while empathizing with the unhappy customers. One of the best investments of a designer's time is to book a recurring one-hour meeting with one or more customer support representatives and shadow them as they take calls. They are a fountain of knowledge when it comes to the user experience issues that need to be resolved. Additionally, they generally know the product better than a lot of the designers. Listening to actual customer calls is one of the most eye-opening and humbling experiences a designer can have. There's nothing like hearing the frustration in a customer's voice when they can't figure out how to perform a simple task to put design decisions into perspective. Hearing the defeated tone of another, asking for help to cancel their account, will most certainly make you reconsider the use of a dark pattern! People's voices carry emotion in a way that no data, spreadsheet, or empirical knowledge can replace.

SEARCH FOR PEOPLE WHO HATE YOUR PRODUCT

A second very humbling experience, and instant ego-killer, is to do a web search for this query: "I hate" + "<name of your product>."

The painful truth that will come out of this query is much better than blissful ignorance. We would even suggest that you create a group for all designers at your company and subscribe it to a Google Alert on this query. This will send everyone in the group an email every time someone mentions that they hate your product or website. We bet this will help the team monitor what changes are working, and what parts of the product need improvement.

A third way of gathering real pain points is to look for unofficial groups and forums that are not curated by your company. There are tons of communities that are built around different products: look for Facebook groups, Quora questions, Twitter searches, subreddits, LinkedIn groups, Google+ Communities, specialized blogs, etc. A community manager is a great resource to help to uncover these communities. The important part is to join them silently, not with the intent of answering all of the questions. Even better, try going undercover. You will be surprised by what users are really saying when they don't know who is listening.

QUANTITATIVE VERSUS QUALITATIVE: GOING ABOVE AND BEYOND LIKERT SCALES

Obviously, we recommend that everyone perform user tests. However, we realize that testing alone is not sufficient. We have witnessed many occasions where the designers observed a certain behavior during tests, but failed to resurface it in a meaningful way during product meetings. The result is predictable. Decisions are made with the data presented to the stakeholders. Therefore, presenting "soft data," such as emotions, is crucial to make our customer's voices heard and avoid causing them emotional pain.

Many companies like using Likert scales in their customer surveys. Likert scales are questions typically formatted with five possible answers, from "strongly disagree" to "strongly agree" (see Figure 6-1). They are very useful to quickly capture the intensity of a respondent's feeling toward a subject. Because they are so familiar to everyone, easy to answer, and fast to compile, Likert scales tend to be overused in user research. This is true of all quantitative measures collected during user research, including the average time to task completion, conversion rate, etc. As much as these can be useful, they should never be the only results collected and presented to stakeholders.

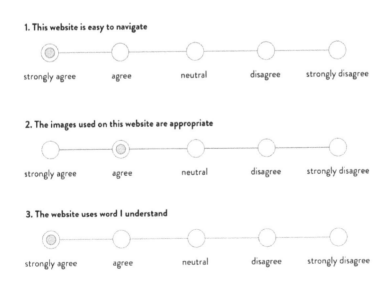

FIGURE 6-1.
Likert scales are commonly used in customer surveys for their convenience

When observing people using a product, the data collected won't always fit nicely on a scale, no matter how convenient that is to put in a PowerPoint presentation. Raw data from observations can, and should, be presented in a variety of ways: descriptions of the user's emotional journey, a list of emojis presenting the emotional states as the user performs a task, candid observations, notes, quotes, and even sketchnotes (see Figure 6-2). These results are way more engaging and more likely to create empathy than a list of graphs and charts. Actually, research shows that our brains can be analytical and empathetic, but not at the same time.[1] A team at Case Western Reserve University studied the way our brain physiology limits simultaneous use of both analytical and empathetic networks. Here's an excerpt from the report:[2]

> How could a CEO be so blind to the public relations fiasco his cost-cutting decision has made?
>
> When the analytic network is engaged, our ability to appreciate the human cost of our action is repressed. At rest, our brains cycle between the social and analytical networks. But when presented with a task, healthy adults engage the appropriate neural pathway, the researchers found. The study shows for the first time that we have a built-in neural constraint on our ability to be both empathetic and analytic at the same time.

Accordingly, if you want to engage your team on an emotional level and create empathy toward your users, it is important not to overwhelm them with hard data. We suggest creating two parts in your design findings presentation. Start with your quantitative findings: the number of customer service tickets, results from Likert scales, the time to completion of different tasks, the error count, the conversion numbers, a cost-benefit analysis, and analytics from Google or other platforms. Then, present the qualitative data: customer journeys, Plutchik's wheel

---

1   Case Western Reserve University. "Empathy Represses Analytic Thought, and Vice Versa." EurekAlert, October 30, 2012, *http://www.eurekalert.org/pub_releases/2012-10/cwru-era103012.php.*

2   Jack, Anthony I., Abigail Dawson, Katelyn Begany, Regina L. Leckie, Kevin Barry, Angela Ciccia, and Abraham Snyder. "fMRI Reveals Reciprocal Inhibition Between Social and Physical Cognitive Domains." *NeuroImage* (2013): 385–401. doi:10.1016/j. neuroimage.2012.10.061

of emotions (that we will describe later), notes from observations during user tests, findings from interviews with customer service representatives, etc. Again, from the same study:

> "You'll never get by without both networks," Jack continued. "You don't want to favor one, but cycle efficiently between them, and employ the right network at the right time."

FIGURE 6-2.
Sketchnote from an interview (image courtesy of Elyse Viotto)

Remember that the CEO of a company has to be highly analytical to keep the business afloat. Your responsibility is to act as a moral compass, making sure the human aspect is taken into consideration when making decisions. That way, no one gets stuck in an analytic way of thinking. User research brings the human element into the analytical environment of business. *In a data-informed, data-driven era, our voice is more important than ever.* The following section will give you tools to gather and present this data in the most effective ways.

Learn to Recognize Emotions

In order to collect "soft" data, we need to be able to understand and recognize it. Unfortunately, we tend to be pretty bad at naming, recognizing, noting, and sharing emotions that we perceive in our testers and customers. Here are some quick lists of verbal and nonverbal signs that help with emotion identification.

Verbal cues to listen out for include:

- The tone of voice—is it aggressive, evasive, embarrassed, cynical, confused, bitter, angry, or passive?

- The words used to describe their actions. A user who mentions that they "have to enter the same information *again*" might not understand why they have to retype their password to confirm it, for example. Make sure, when taking notes, that you put emphasis on these words that act as modulators.

- Sighs. The number of sighs you hear speaks for itself. Once you start actually counting them, you may find they are a lot more frequent than you would have imagined. Come up with a sign to quickly jot down when a user sighs, without having to spell it out. We like the tilde (~) because it's not used regularly.

- Laughter. A laugh can also betray a feeling that the interface is acting "stupidly." Users may scoff at confusing choices, reactions, or requirements of the software.

Also look and listen for nonverbal cues—visible or audible signs of irritation or any variations in behavior, such as:

- Suddenly typing louder on the keyboard after making an error

- Rolling their eyes

- Making circular motions with the cursor on the screen, as if they had lost it

- Nervous tics such as replacing their glasses, touching a ring, running their hands through their hair, etc.

- Redness in the face or in the neck

- Change of position on the chair

- Sighing, grunting, or other noises

- Scrunching of the nose or eyes

DECODING EXPRESSIONS OF EMOTION AND BODY LANGUAGE

There are seven universal facial emotions (disgust, anger, fear, sadness, happiness, surprise, and contempt) that can be expressed in different ways: through macroexpressions (typically lasting between ½ second and 4 seconds) or microexpressions (involuntary, of less than

½ second).[3] We don't always accurately recognize the common macro-expressions on people's faces. Learning to decode more evasive expressions makes a designer more sensitive and empathetic to the range of emotions that are actually felt.

Many think that they can't decode microexpressions, but with little training, it's very easy to develop basic recognition skills. Learning to diagnose what people are feeling is extremely powerful as a designer. All the basic emotions can be mixed together. Learn them. Understand their different intensities and variations. It's only when you know something that you can design with it in mind.

PRESENTING THESE OBSERVATIONS

There's nothing like presenting movie clips of someone frustrated with a service to instantly create empathy toward them. We find that a five-minute video that shows actual footage of a user's struggles works great. To gather this video, you want to make sure you film both the screen and the user's face during the tests. Watching these clips can make people uncomfortable, but this awkwardness is important.

MAPPING EMOTIONAL DATA

Once you've observed actual people using your product and collected a bunch of information about their feelings, it's important to record those findings in an appropriate manner. To do so, we suggest presenting the data on *maps of users' emotions*. These can be very powerful when presenting issues to different stakeholders.

Such a map can also serve as a template to gather data, by simply showing it to testers when asking them for feedback about your product. It can be used as a way to quantify and measure qualitative elements.

Plutchik's wheel

As a base, we suggest using Robert Plutchik's emotion wheel:[4] its greatest benefit lies in its simplicity. There are a lot of different theories about emotions, but most of these agree that they manifest in different

---

3 *The Nature of Things.* "Body Language Decoded." Written and directed by Geoff D'Eon, CBC-TV, February 16, 2017, *http://www.cbc.ca/natureofthings/episodes/body-language-decoded.*

4 Plutchik, Robert. *Emotions and Life: Perspectives from Psychology, Biology, and Evolution.* Washington, DC: American Psychological Association, 2002.

intensities and that the basic emotions can be combined with others to create new emotional states. For example, on Plutchik's wheel, a mix of acceptance and apprehension creates submission. It's really helpful to build a better understanding of the whole spectrum and to put customers' experiences into words. Also, imagine how powerful a proper recording of emotions is compared to a superficial one: "Four of our users were angry" is much less precise than "Two users were angry, one showed signs of rage, and the last one was right at the border of disgust and loathing" (see Figure 6-3). This capacity for describing emotional states with precision and granularity is a great advantage for designers.

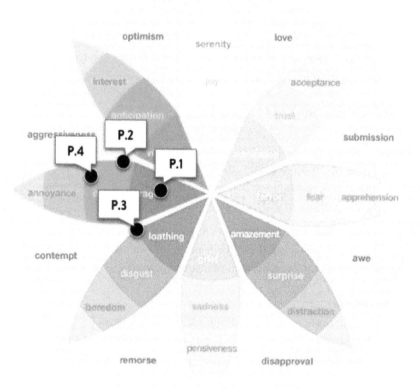

FIGURE 6-3.
Participants mapping their emotions on Plutchik's wheel

Customer journeys

Another great way to map emotions and present them to your stake-holders is by creating a customer journey that highlights the emotional states at every step. A customer journey created with the whole team becomes a key piece in building alignment with and empathy toward the user. Invite every stakeholder of the project for a half-day activity; the more the merrier!

Many customer journeys (or experience maps) are created only as a way to make an inventory of every task performed by a user. This should never be the sole reason to create one. It's important that for every major activity or task listed, the key emotion felt by the user is highlighted. This will put emphasis on the pain points and can be used as inspiration for design opportunities. Make sure to highlight the areas of greatest opportunity, and that it aims at seeing the experience through your customer's eyes, not yours.

There are many ways of creating customer journeys. We suggest the excellent canvas proposed by This Is Service Design Thinking (see Figure 6-4).

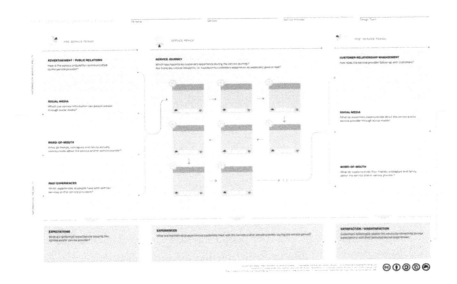

FIGURE 6-4.

The customer journey canvas by This Is Service Design Thinking (*http:// thisisservicedesignthinking.com*)

Adaptive Path, the user experience design and consulting firm, also has a wonderful and free guide that helps with mapping experiences (see Figure 6-5). Finally, for a complete overview of the different journeys, diagrams, and blueprints that exist out there, see *Mapping Experiences,* by James Kalbach (O'Reilly).

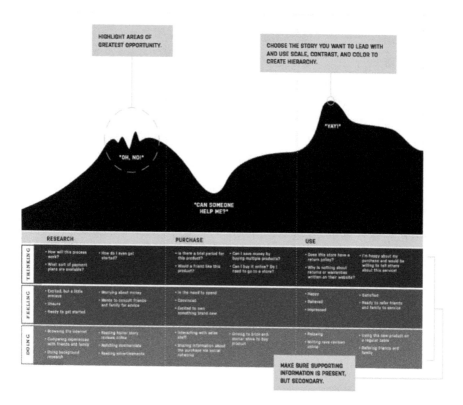

FIGURE 6-5.

Example of an experience map from Adaptive Path's Guide to Experience Mapping (*http://mappingexperiences.com*)

One of the main challenges in implementing the use of empathy in the workplace can be other people's perception of it. Some view empathy as "hokey," "touchy-feely," or just a feel-good practice that doesn't have any effect on real work. As we know, it's a critical tool in building the right product—so how can we convince others to adopt it? The key is...empathy, but I'm sure you knew that was coming. Where are your stakeholders coming from? What do they value? For some the key may be pointing to case studies or previous projects where it was used effectively. For others, perhaps it's data: you can explain to them that empathy gives context to data. You can also explain how it is used effectively in very successful companies like Google, IDEO, Facebook, etc. Lastly, if you don't fully feel confident in utilizing empathy, be up front with your team. Let them know it's something you want to work toward, something you've read about and would like to test. Ask them to give it a try, and mention that you are looking for their feedback to make this exercise better.

Conclusion

In this chapter we have encouraged empathizing with users in order to create apt design solutions. There is, however, a risk when we attempt to empathize with users without an anchor in user research. We think we know what might motivate users, how they might react, what they might think, and what they might do. However, if this empathy is not founded in user research, then it is most likely a false empathy where we insert our own thoughts and preferences in the place of what real users actually want and experience. We tend to trick our brains into thinking other people want what we want. This was shown in a study that appeared in the *Journal of Marketing Research*.[5] There were two groups of marketing managers. One group, the control, were asked to predict customers' desires and to complete a survey assessing their own empathy levels. The second group had the same tasks, but were first asked to be empathetic by describing a typical customer and imagining what that person might think or do. One of the researchers, Professor Johannes Hattula, described the results in an interview with the *Harvard Business Review*:

> The effect was consistent. The more empathetic managers were, the more they used their personal preferences to predict what customers would want.[6]

---

5   Hattula, Johannes D., Walter Herzog, Darren W. Dahl, and Sven Reinecke. "Managerial Empathy Facilitates Egocentric Predictions of Consumer Preferences." *Journal of Marketing Research* 52:2 (April 2015): 235–252.

6   Berinato, Scott. "Putting Yourself in the Customer's Shoes Doesn't Work: An Interview with Johannes Hattula." *Harvard Business Review* 93:3 (2015): 34–35. Available at *https:// hbr.org/2015/03/putting-yourself-in-the-customers-shoes-doesnt-work*.

Practicing empathy encouraged the managers to inject their own preferences and biases into their evaluation of what users would want and how they would behave. This happens often and in many companies. We know a lot about our users, so we think we know what they will think and do. We are all familiar with the old design adage "you are not the user," but we think that knowing about the user allows us to avoid this common trap. This research shows the crux of that mindset: thinking *"on behalf of the user"* is still designing for yourself. This is dangerous, not only because it can mean we end up designing solutions that miss their mark, but also because we may start ignoring evidence that contradicts us. Once again, Professor Hattula:

> Another key finding that should get people's attention is that the more empathetic the managers were, the more they ignored the market research on customers that we provided them.

The dangers of this thinking are twofold. First, we fool ourselves into thinking we know what users want, and then we block out contrary evidence. It's a recipe for disaster—one that many of us continue to cook up as we work hard on meeting deadlines and stakeholders' demands. The key to avoiding this trap is letting the research guide your understanding of what users think and do. That is why the information in this chapter is critical to your business's success, not only in terms of avoiding harming your users, but in guiding you in the right direction to truly meet their needs.

Key Takeaways

1. Knowing that people hate your product is much better than living in blissful ignorance.

2. If we want to engage our teams on an emotional level and create empathy toward our users, it is important not to overwhelm them with hard data.

3. When observing people using a product, the data collected shouldn't always fit nicely on a scale, no matter how convenient this is to go in a PowerPoint presentation.

4. There are seven universal facial emotions (disgust, anger, fear, sadness, happiness, surprise, and contempt) that can be expressed in different ways: through macroexpressions (typically lasting between ½ second and 4 seconds) or microexpressions (involuntary, of less than ½ second).

5. A proper recording of emotions is powerful compared to a superficial one: "Four of our users were angry" is much less precise than "Two users were angry, one showed signs of rage, and the last one was right at the border of disgust and loathing." This capacity of describing emotional states with precision and granularity is a great advantage for designers.

6. A great way to map emotions and present them to your team is by creating a customer journey that highlights the emotional states at every step.

Interview with Erika Hall of Mule Design

The following is a transcription of an audio recording of an interview with Erika Hall of Mule Design.

1. Where does design make the biggest impact in our lives?

There are two or three different ways it does. One, the big one I talk about sometimes, is the opportunity cost. It's not that designers contribute to something that is evil, too much of the time. The thing that happens more often is that there are all of these real problems, and this is why I started writing, working, and researching a lot of the startup culture, is that people don't pick real problems. What happens is all of these really smart, talented people waste so much time doing stupid things that they never get to a real issue. I don't just mean doing something for the public good, I just mean making a viable product or service. So I think waste is itself is immoral. It's like, "Oh, we could we be doing something useful but instead we are playing into this short-term venture shell game with our time and our skills as opposed to really asking ourselves 'Well, what are we trying to accomplish and are we working to make sure it is successful?'" So there's this waste aspect to it.

2. What is the purpose of technology for you?

Technology doesn't really have a purpose. Everything we do is a technology in a certain sense. Reading and writing is a technology in a certain sense.

It's all about what you put it toward. Technology is inherently a tool. What is a hammer for?

3. What is the purpose of design?

Before you can have design you have to have a mature craft. People build houses for a certain number of years and then architecture is a thing. People create newspapers for a certain number of years and then graphic design is a thing. There's no design until you have a mature craft. All design is is a higher order of thinking about a craft or about a process. People conflate design and craft too much. If you're talking about design, then to really do design what you've got to do is to think through the implications of any design you are making. Because the idea is that as a designer you are participating in or leading this considered process. So you can't really call yourself a designer unless you are thinking about it. Otherwise you are just making a thing. If somebody comes up to you and gives you the schematics and they are like, "Make this dating app, give it an appealing interface but it's going to do these things and have this functionality"—if you are just going to take those instructions and do the surface of the app, I don't know to what extent, if you just take those marching orders, you can even consider yourself a designer. There's this craft but if you are doing it unconsciously that's how we get bad design. People who have the skills and intelligence to do things consciously and intentionally don't do things consciously and intelligently. They just use their skills to fulfill someone else's plan.

4. What would be your advice to designers to avoid that?

I think the best way is by applying intention, to really think, "I really mean to bring this into the world. I really sign onto this." No longer seeing themselves in this passive, order-taking role. People are weighting the influence of design and designers more. So we have to get out of this mindset of "I just have to take everything that comes my way and I'm going to apply my own materials or process to it." If I'm going to be out there putting new things into the world, what's my point of view? I've been asked in the past, "What makes a good designer?" and it's a strong point of view, even more so than really excellent skills. There are people with a combination of those two things, a strong point of view and excellent skills. For example, you look at Paul Rand the logo designer, he had both those things: excellent technical skills and a very strong point of view. When designers think about progressing in their career, skill is one part of it but figuring out what your point of view is is the other part of it.

5. What should make up that point of view?

It all comes from understanding the implications of what you are doing and having that vision of "How do I want to use my skills to change the world?" Even in small ways. To do this you don't have to be a famous designer or anything like that but you just have to apply that intentionality in the problems you choose to take on and how you choose to apply your skills. Every design embodies a set of values, so first it's about being clear on your own values. You can come out, as a designer, and say "My value is making this money for myself," or you could say "My value is about clarifying information for people." And that is one of the greatest powers of design, is to understand and clarify meanings, so people out in the world don't make bad choices for themselves because things are unclear. It is empowering everybody in their own decision making. That is something good design can help people with.

6. How is Mule Design living out the point of view you have?

Well, we have a very strong point of view but a big part of our work is the writing we do, and we are starting to do a lot of training, in addition to taking on projects for clients, to help people and support people because this something that is not taught in schools. You look at a school like RISD and they actually have a philosophy department and have classes in this, but a lot of times if you go to a "design school" their teaching is graphic design, history of design, how to lay things out, interface design principles, and at no point do they give students the skills to think through the larger considerations. That's what we are doing through our "Dear Design Student" series (*https://deardesignstudent.com*) and our books. What the various blogging and writings do is help give young designers tools. You are set out there and you think, "Oh I am just lucky to have a job, I'll do whatever" or "I will do projects that seem fun," but you don't think "I don't think this is right but I don't have the vocabulary to articulate why this isn't right" or "I don't have the status to push back on this." I think all designers should be able to have these skills. Designers leave school with the ability to critique each other's work. You have to defend your work but in a very small scope. I would like designers to be able to defend and critique their work while keeping in mind the world at large is your client. Engaging with people is part of the job and that is something that a lot of designers are not trained to do. They think "I design with my hands" but you don't. You design with your mind and your intellect. Your hands are secondary, it is just a way to create artifacts for expression. That's what we like to do: helping other designers to recognize their own power, and to not just participate in a dialogue about what various decisions mean but to lead and facilitate that dialogue.

7. What is something practical designers can do that will help them make the right ethical choices?

When people think about research they think, "I am going out to find new information." When designers research, what that really means is establishing and understanding the context. Looking at the context your work is in: how users currently behave, the competitive context, looking at the wider world, etc. So it first starts with what people traditionally call research which is background information so you can understand the full problem. Don't let people cut that out of the process. I don't care how innovative what you are working on is, it has to fit into the real world. If you are working for somebody and they are not ethical, get another job!

8. What is your advice to nondesigners who are building products?

Know what your values are and know why you are doing it. Know what it means to you to be successful and then with that in mind, you can better evaluate things that might feel good to do but are irrational. A great example is Stewart Butterfield, the founder of Slack. He also has a Masters in Philosophy. He is a very smart and thoughtful person. I think the way he goes about things and makes decisions is a good model as a designer. There was that horrible "gamification" trend going for a while, but what Stewart has done, a few times now, is found a gaming company, make an interesting game, and then figure out which part of the game is an interesting product. It is totally backwards from the way everyone else does it. He did it with Flickr and he did it with Slack. That was so much smarter than the way anyone else does it. What part of this interesting social interaction could be useful as a product? Most people are so driven by anxiety and fear and wanting to copy other people that they make things that fail, as opposed to having the confidence to trust this process, want something higher and long lasting.

[7]

What We Can Do

THE HARD PART IS not convincing you. Chances are, if you picked up this book, and read it all the way to here, you are already convinced of the importance of good design decisions. If you want a new house, it's twice the work to choose land with a shabby house already on it. You either have to demolish the old one or find all the differences between the old house and your plan and make all the required changes. It is much easier to demolish the old one and build from scratch. It's the same with changing the minds of people and the way things are done. You first have to demolish the belief system they already have and then build up the new ideas from the ground up. The easiest part of what we can do is acting on what we believe. We have deconstructed the myth of how design affects people's lives (or rather, doesn't) and hopefully convinced you that it does. Now the hard part will be convincing those who aren't converted and challenging what is already in place: your boss's beliefs about the value of design, the politics at work, and of course national politics. This is very difficult, but the good news is that change is possible, and once that change gets going, it goes fast.

What We All Can Do

Before we speak specifically to designers, we want to address anyone else who might be reading this and is interested in what part they can play. This advice may also be shared with friends and colleagues.

The biggest enemy of change is complacency, and it takes more effort to change something that already exists—thus, we often leave it be and put our efforts into our everyday activities. Remember, big changes come from small ones. Do something every day, every week, and change will come.

VOTE

Being an engaged citizen gives you great power for change. In our democratic societies, we each have a say in how things are done. With voter turnout rates being only about 50% in the US and just over 80% in the countries with the highest turnout,[1] just showing up will give you more say than those who do not.

Believe it or not, there are laws about user experience, many of which are already in place. In the US, for example, there is a law—Section 508 of the Rehabilitation Act of 1973 (29 U.S.C. § 794 (d))—that requires all government websites be accessible for those with various disabilities. This helps ensure that all citizens interacting with their government electronically (their term!) will not be excluded.

The problem is often not just in getting the law passed, which can be a battle on its own, but in the proper enforcement of that law. For example, the law mandating that electronic health records be backed by user research doesn't work because there is no way to properly certify that the user research has been done in a standardized way. We need to push for better usability laws and make sure they can be properly enforced.

SPEAK UP

Oftentimes we suffer in silence; we anguish over what should be done but say nothing. We assume the response we would receive from those above us would be negative. However, we have found that the act of simply speaking up can have an immediate and profound effect. Many people are simply oblivious to the effect of bad design. They see it from a distinctive perspective and can't see how confusing it is for others. Other times they get lost in the day-to-day and don't give design the attention it deserves. Always assume that they are well-meaning people, and the act of simply raising the issue can be enough to get them to fix it. If they don't see your point right away, it will at least raise their awareness about the problem. Don't stop at the first attempt! The best designer is a broken record. When others hear about the same issue again and again, they *will* come to understand its importance over time.

---

1 DeSilver, Drew. "U.S. Voter Turnout Trails Most Developed Countries." Pew Research Center, August 2, 2016, *http://pewrsr.ch/2aSktkE*.

Keeping these issues fresh in the minds of those in positions of influence is very important. It can seem like there is no movement, but over time, they can be won over.

When you see bad design at work that might hurt people, *raise your hand*. When you spend two hours on a government website trying to figure how to make a payment, speak up and email them. When you see dangerously designed software at a hospital, write to management. When you hear about a friend getting harassed online, complain to the support team. Every time we speak up, we shine a light into the shadows, and with that illumination will come change as people recognize the issues we raise as important problems that require action.

SUPPORT OTHERS

As we've mentioned, creating real change is a difficult and lengthy task. It can often feel discouraging and seem like our efforts are being dumped into an empty void. We need each other's encouragement and support to make this work. When one person speaks up, make sure you support them. When you see someone at your company pushing for better usability, encourage them and let them know they are doing a great job. When you see someone running an organization that is creating change, write to them and tell them you appreciate their work. *Words of encouragement are a beautiful, simple tool.* Simply recognizing someone's efforts gives them more fuel for their passion.

Another way to help someone else who is creating change is giving financially. For example, when given a choice, buy from a company that is accessible and let them know why you chose them! Money = energy, and by giving you allow them to do more of what they are doing well.

SHARE GOOD EXAMPLES

Another simple and effortless way to help the efforts of others is to share what they do. When you come across an organization, an event, or a website that is creating change, share it with everyone in your sphere of influence. You know the drill: share it on social media, email interested friends, connect the people running it with like-minded people who might be able to help them, and vote up their posts on social news websites. This will give them more visibility, help them with marketing, and might ring a bell for their competitors.

START YOUR OWN COMPANY

Sometimes the best way to create change is to make something better than the status quo. In the tech world, we call this "disruption." A new player comes into the market and flips everything upside down because they can do it so much better, and the old players are too big and clunky to change fast enough to stop them from eating up the entire market. It's the survival of the fittest. If a species doesn't adapt to the changing environment, it dies out, and its loss is another's gain.

Today, it is ever more realistic for a small group of people to start something new and take on much larger players. Startups everywhere are challenging billion-dollar companies to do better. If you are passionate about wanting to see a particular part of this problem change and see an opportunity in the market, then start something! We need entrepreneurs out there who care about the user experience and can exploit the desperately lacking experiences in many products that are causing harm to people every day. You will have a special advantage as well: users often prefer less functionality if they can get a better experience. Starting a company has never been this accessible, and failing is trendier than ever. You've got nothing to lose!

PRACTICE EMPATHY

The best way to start changing your own behavior, that which may overlook these areas of harm, is to practice empathy. *Sympathy*, feeling pity for the troubles of others, isn't enough to create change within ourselves and our products. *Empathy*, the understanding and sharing of feelings, is required to prevent harming unwillingly. Practicing empathy is not reserved for designers, but in order to design better products we need to truly understand the people that use them. We need a deep understanding of their perspectives, needs, and wants. For example, when Jonathan had to design a new intake process, he came up against an interesting challenge: it is common for some people not to have an email account. To a designer who grew up in Silicon Valley, this was hard to understand. It might have been tempting to leave those people out of the experience he was designing. But when trying to understand the situation, he learned that these users had been left behind by the technology boom. For many, the cost of learning to use a computer is judged too high because they get by just fine. There are other edge cases where people will not have an email address; for example, a child.

Knowing all of this, he designed a way to accommodate offline intake forms, by allowing staff to input the answers from the paper form. Taking on these challenges with empathy leads to better solutions.

EVERYONE IS A DESIGNER

For designers, what we're designing often ends up being the interface of a product, but for non-designers, it can be so many things. Are you an employee in a restaurant who has realized the menu on the website is in Flash, thus not accessible? Or a salesperson in a car dealership who feels its advertising choices might be hurting and excluding people? Perhaps you are an executive planning the direction of a company—will it focus on the users' needs, leave anyone out, or cause harm? Even creating a spreadsheet can involve designing for others who may use it. We can all keep in mind our end users and make sure that we don't just "get the job done," but go the extra mile to make the experience of others better.

What Designers Can Do

We designers have a critical role to play in protecting people from bad design. We have the knowledge (hopefully!), and with it comes the responsibility to do the right thing for our users. It's not always easy, but we must do our very best in every situation because people need design now more than ever. As technology takes over more of our lives, there is an ever-greater need for people to be able to understand and use it.

WORK WHERE YOU ARE NEEDED

If you have read this far, then perhaps you are one of the designers who care enough to do what it will take to create change. We need people like you in the areas of business that haven't traditionally valued design but desperately need to. It's a rough gig, but we need you, and it is very fulfilling! That might mean taking less appealing jobs: ones where perhaps your friends might not recognize or use the product you're working on, but where your efforts will make a real difference. We need designers like you in healthcare, where aging infrastructure, bloated organizational structures, and business ties all stand in the way of better design benefiting patients and the hospital staff caring for them. We need you in government, where bureaucracy, lack of funding, and obfuscated processes will be standing in your way. We need you in education, the sciences, aeronautics, the automobile industry, and even business-to-business software. Each has its own set of challenges waiting to be broken down, with the potential of huge gains for its users. *Our time is valuable, and as we spend much of our time at work we should choose a place where we can make a difference.* If you feel strongly about protecting users from harm, opening access to technology, and making the world a more pleasant place through design, then these challenges belong to you, and all the future victories as well.

LEARN TO RAISE YOUR VOICE

Speaking up has a profoundly simple way of changing things. Changing the unsaid into something tangible. When you speak up, the issue you raised has to be addressed. It must enter the minds of those involved and be considered. Even if it's dismissed time and again, it will eventually start to materialize as an important issue; it will be brought into the light and get the attention it deserves. Your boss might even surprise you. Jonathan remembers agonizing over how his own boss would choose to use dark patterns in some of the purchase flows his company was designing. After the meetings, the designers would complain to each other about it. However, once he spoke up about it and called it a dark pattern, and gave data to support his claim that the practice should be changed, the boss very happily obliged.

No one with good intentions can deny good data. Most often, they don't know what they are doing is harmful to users, and simply bringing up the subject can illuminate it for them. Speak up in a meeting, send a thoughtful email, give a presentation to your company; raise awareness of the issues whatever way you can. (We assume here that you have a boss—if you are in position of leadership, impose change on your staff!)

TAKE A STAND

If the harm that is being caused is significant and serious enough, then simply speaking up isn't enough. You must take a stand. As the designer of a product, *you are responsible for the work you do.* If the harm being caused is serious, then you cannot let it pass by. Take a stand. It can feel scary risking your employment, but it's scarier to risk your morality. We can only imagine what the designers of some of the examples given in this book might feel like, knowing that their products have killed or injured people. Life's too short to make compromises on your morality—there will be a next job, and perhaps the period in between will be rough, but you can feel good knowing you took a stand. And as we mentioned before, managers respect people with convictions. Hey, your own manager might even surprise you!

BE A GREAT DESIGNER

The world doesn't need more people who make pretty interfaces—it needs great designers. We need people who thoughtfully craft experiences. To create good designs, we have to first be good designers. Here are some tips on how to be a better designer.

1. Be a world-class communicator.

This is true for many jobs, but especially for designers: your ability to communicate will be the deciding factor in your success. In every facet of a designer's job, good communication plays a key role: discussing project requirements with stakeholders, pitching clients, brainstorming ideas with your team, design critiques, and of course knowing how to communicate with users through the interfaces you design. You can't get away from it—all the genius trapped in your brain will stay there if you don't know how to share it and sell it. Don't get stuck only thinking about how to communicate with your users. Before you can advocate for them, you must also communicate with the team around you to get them to buy into the vision you have. Communication is one of the most fruitful skills you can spend your time improving.

In his book *Articulating Design Decisions* (O'Reilly), Tom Greever gives great advice for designers. He explains the process of preparing for and presenting your designs. More importantly, Greever argues that designers need to understand stakeholder perspectives, and learn how to empathize with them in order to achieve our goals. If you are shy, try joining a Toastmasters group (Toastmasters is a nonprofit educational organization that teaches public speaking and leadership skills through a worldwide network of clubs; see *https://www.toastmasters. org/About*). Challenge yourself to give a presentation internally, or, even better, at a regional meet-up. If you are up for the challenge, apply to give talks at larger events. Look for events that aren't only design-focused; they often have a "varia" track that regroups topics that their guests might find interesting.

2. Use the user-centered design methodology.

Anyone can design; all it takes is rendering your intentions (to reference Jared Spool's pithy definition). However, being a good designer requires you to also be user-centric. Since we usually serve a business, it's easy to get lulled into designing solutions that meet business needs first and then doing our very best to shoehorn the users' needs in (or at least soften the blow). The conundrum is that it's better business to be user-focused. After all, your users are ultimately the ones paying you. Everyone has a boss (unless you are the boss, in which case you are already applying a UCD methodology, aren't you?). Your boss might be the one writing you a check, but someone writes their check, right? Start with user needs first and fit in business needs after that.

More importantly, learn about the UCD methodology. Look for books on the subject—we suggest *Understanding Your Users* by Kathy Baxter and Catherine Courage and *User-Centered Design Stories* by Carol Righi and Janice James (both from Elsevier/Morgan Kaufmann).

3. Use data as ammunition.

A designer without data is blind. Whenever possible, back up design decisions with data. In the best cases, you have real data from your users; at other times it will be a hypothesis based on best practices, experience, or observed behavior. The higher quality the ammo, the bigger the bang. Decide up front what data you will need, and be able to get, at the start and end of your project. Data can inform good design and validate it. This way of thinking, paired with good communication, can transform your company's perspective on design. Learn more about data-informed design by watching the talk "Data-Informed Design" by Jen Matson (*http://oreil.ly/2oFkGCm*).

4. Keep a student's mindset.

Just like everything else in nature, if you're not growing, you rot. Take every opportunity to learn and never let your pride get in the way. Take on an attitude of learning, so when you fail or succeed at a project, you are always aware of the lessons. Learn from others. If someone solves an issue you had, make them explain it to you. When you see others succeed, stop and think what factors led to that success. We learn so much in a single day but fail to take note. Keep a notebook with your insights and key learnings every day.

It also pays to be connected to the design community, reading what other designers are thinking, keeping up to date on the latest news and tools, and learning from what other designers are doing. Here are some of our personal favorite resources to get you started:

- *designernews.co*
- *medium.com*
- *smashingmagazine.com*
- *uxbooth.com*
- *uxmag.com*

Gobble up all the information you can, but remember that you must also pair learning with doing. There is no better way to cement the lessons you observe than to put them into practice. Even after decades in the industry, there are always lessons that can be learned. Even the tallest redwoods continue to grow, centuries on.

5. Teach and mentor others.

A great designer will multiply their learning by turning around and teaching it to others. You can share the why behind your design decisions not only to show the reasoning behind them, but also to share that knowledge so they too can use it. At a minimum, this helps people understand what you do. It can help an organization in so many different ways as people use the information. Teaching can also reinforce your learning and solidify a lesson in your mind so you don't forget it in the future. Companies who hire these teaching designers will get a great return on their investment, as the entire team learns from each other and grows.

Once you've been designing for a while (and if you have the opportunity), try to mentor a new designer. You will both benefit immensely from the mentor–mentee relationship.

6. Polish your process.

It's common knowledge that baking is a science, and every step of the process affects the outcome. Design is similar. Having a process in place helps you plan better, make sure the right things get done at the right time, and get a predictable outcome. The outcome won't always be the same—you can experiment and improve on it—but it will be dependable, so you can experiment by changing specific factors in the process and know exactly how the outcome was affected. If you don't have time to fix your process, then you are moving backward. A good designer can only do good work with the right process in place.

What is the right process? There are many models out there, but they all include some critical elements:

1. Understanding the problem (collecting user research, requirements from stakeholders, relevant data, etc.)

2. Exploring concepts (sketching, making wireframes and prototypes, etc.)

3. Building (UI, code, style guides, etc.)

4. Validating and analyzing (more user research, understanding data, and iterating)

The Design Process by Karl Aspelund (Fairchild Books) is a good starting point. *Design with Intent* by Dan Lockton (O'Reilly) is another good read.

7. Take your time.

We've learned over the years that great design takes time. A very senior designer with lots of experience can perhaps take less time, but time is necessary to take a design from good to great. In our experience, companies often try to rush through the design and ideation phases. This is a perilous mistake, and often the project must backtrack in order to correct its direction. It takes a lot of additional time for the work to be redone or fixed. The old adage "Measure twice, cut once" applies when designing products. When we don't take the time to plan and ideate, we waste the precious resources of the company. As a designer, you may not have control over this, but at least take all the time you're allowed. Ask for a delivery day, perhaps even negotiate more time, and then plan so you can take more time thinking about the problem in detail and exploring different solutions. We so often live "hand to mouth" and deliver designs in the quickest window possible. Try instead to take all the time you can (remaining mindful of deadlines) and put the emphasis on the planning stages. Developing empathy is not something that happens magically; it takes invested time.

8. Be engaged.

Don't be just another cog in the machine—be engaged. This means understanding the people you work with. It means caring enough to push back, being engaged at every step of the process and striving to improve. It is asking "why" and "how," repeating what you hear so people know you hear them. In essence, it's taking your job seriously and reaching outside your portion of the product development process.

9. Take a step back.

This is yet another aspect that separates good designers from great ones. We all need course corrections, and we all definitely need inspiration from time to time. Find times where you can stop what you are doing and take a step back. If it is a larger project, take a moment, perhaps midway, to step back and look at the project as a whole. Painters do this to make sure the painting comes together and that they don't get lost in the details. We need that context too. How will this feature work in the overall experience? How will it interact with feature B? Taking a step back will help you make important course corrections and do better work.

You will also find yourself feeling burned out every now and then. Don't worry; every designer goes through these phases. Design is a draining job, and sometimes we need to take a bigger step back and look at our careers. Where am I headed? What can I do differently to reignite my passion and fill my tank? You can switch projects or companies if need be; you can learn new skills, and take up your own projects. Your career, like any project, can be planned, designed, and tested and is an iterative project. A designer that is disengaged and struggles staying motivated won't be in the best position to do their best work and prevent harming their users.

10. Branch out.

We have found that the most successful designers are an insatiably curious lot. Growing up, they were the kids always asking why, and they never stopped. Designers have the ability to take unrelated ideas and find the connections to the current problem. Designers should branch out and find hobbies and interests outside of design. Some are directly applicable—programming, business, public speaking, or calligraphy—but so many others can find their own unique way in informing your designs and providing fresh perspectives on future problems.

Learn about other topics that interest you. Study classical animation, learn how to craft a chair, or how algorithms work. We find the more branches you have going out, the better. It gives you a better perspective on the world you will be designing for. In turn, you can bring your experiences and fresh perspectives into those fields that desperately need it.

11. Contribute.

Open source isn't just for programmers. Everyone can contribute to open source software. Designers who know how to do frontend coding can contribute to a wide range of visual and usability improvements, and bring a layer of professionalism to the presentation of the site. Designers who don't can help to add more descriptive HTML to increase the accessibility of a project. They can also submit bugs that they find and provide detailed feedback. They can help by testing on different platforms, and take part in conversations and arguments. Find out more about this at the Open Design Foundation (*http://opendesign.foundation*).

You can also contribute at a local level by attending municipal meetings, city consultations, city-organized hackathons, etc.

12. Ask who is losing and who is winning.

A useful tool when designing new features is to ask yourself, "Who is winning and who is losing?" If the feature services only the business, then it is a bad feature that will not do well. If only the user is winning, you will gain traction but will not be able to maintain the business through its success. With great design, everyone wins. Seek solutions that represent a win-win. The greatest success will come when you find this overlap. Products that only serve the business are likely to fizzle out or cause harm. By asking this question whenever you set out to design a new feature, you will avoid both.

STOP READING THIS BOOK... (SOON!)

It's time to stop reading and start doing! Go out there and put into practice everything you've learned. In the next chapter, you can read about some great companies who are at the vanguard in fixing many of these issues, and they are a great place to start if you want to get involved. But first, a bit of homework!

Take some time to write an action plan:

1. What are you passionate about?

In this book, we have covered some of the major areas where bad design can have real costs. Think about which of the stories that were shared moved you the most. Explore the topics you care about, and the ones that have affected you or your loved ones. Choose what problem you want to spend your time on.

2. Allocate your time.

Decide how much time you will be able to spend on it. This may be determined by how passionate you are about the area you chose and your own circumstances. You can choose to dedicate a single weekend, or one day a week, or do as much as seeking a job in that area. Whatever you choose, write it down and stick to it. Add it to your phone's alerts, put it on a sticky note near your monitor, write it on the back of your hand—anything to make sure you don't forget!

3. Find an outlet.

There are many places that would benefit from your time: offer your services to a nonprofit you want to help, contribute code to a public project, or even apply for a job at one of the companies listed in the next chapter or another worthwhile organization.

4. Tell a friend.

Last but not least, spread the word! Sharing about the real cost of bad design and how people can get involved in fixing it will accelerate progress. Designers need to hear how they can help, and those in the industry need to hear about the importance of design and how serious the costs can be when it isn't valued appropriately. You can share posts about the cost of bad design, or write them. You can also, of course, point others to our website (*http://www.tragicdesign.com*), where we will be sharing more examples. Sharing is a critical part of making progress in helping everyone understand the importance of design in these vital areas of our lives.

[8]

They Are Doing Good

We have laid out how bad design affects all of us in very real ways. We have recounted many stories of how people have been hurt by bad design. We also have discussed how we can be agents of change and make things better. We want to turn your attention now to the people out there already on the front lines making a difference. People who have seen the need for better design and are doing their part to create a better world for you and I to live in. People who, like us, see the enormous potential design has to broaden the bridge to technology and better serve people's needs. Let me briefly share with you these successes, to show you that you are not alone. Together we can make a difference!

Physical Good

We talk about how bad design can cause physical harm, but here are some examples of people using good design to create physical good!

- Mad*Pow (*http://www.madpow.com*) is a design agency that aims to improve the experiences people have with technology, organizations, and each other. They have set out to change healthcare, and have made huge strides. One of those measures is putting together the annual Healthcare Experience Design (HXD) conference, which brings together thought leaders in design and health to find ways the two can work together to improve the lives of patients. The rest of the year, Mad*Pow is an agency of passionate designers who tackle problems in healthcare, help nonprofits, and take on many other challenges.

- Prescribe Design (*http://www.prescribedesign.com*) is a movement started by cofounders Aaron Sklar and Lenny Naar. Both come from a background in healthcare and are passionate about infusing it with people-centered design to better patients' lives. The main purpose of Prescribe Design is to "merge the conversations in design with those in health, bringing design natives and health-care natives together." They create events, start conversations on social media, and make connections between designers and healthcare providers. These conversations and connections act as catalysts that trigger new ideas, partnerships, and movements of their own.

- Rock Health (*http://www.rockhealth.com*) is a venture group that seeks "to fund and support entrepreneurs working at the intersection of healthcare and technology." They value design heavily, and it's evident in the resources and direction they provide for their portfolio companies. Their mission is "to make healthcare massively better for every human being. We support companies improving the quality, safety, and accessibility of our healthcare system." By funding companies that put these standards first, Rock Health is helping move the industry forward.

- IDEO (*http://www.ideo.org*) is well known for is design prowess but has made its biggest impact with IDEO.org, which serves a multitude of different projects that span many categories here. It has made a big impact in healthcare in developing countries through many small projects. IDEO uses human-centered design to create a big social impact. It also helps engage designers through its Amplify challenge, which poses a question and follows a process where designers can contribute to answering it and executing on it through the open idea platform.

- OXO (*http://www.oxo.com*) is a company that develops tools with the principle of inclusive and universal design. It started when the owner saw his wife was having trouble comfortably holding her vegetable peeler due to arthritis. He designed a better peeler that is now iconic. OXO products have won numerous design awards and are included in the permanent collections of many museums worldwide.

Emotional Good

Bad design causes emotional distress, but good design causes delight and removes stress. Good design promotes positive interactions between people and builds communities. Here are a few examples of organizations making that happen:

- Design for Good (*http://www.aiga.org/design-for-good*) connects AIGA members with socially impactful organizations. From large projects to small, AIGA members donate their time to a wide variety of different causes and competitions.

- UX for Good (*http://www.uxforgood.org*) gets talented designers together to ask really hard questions about social challenges and let loose designers to solve these problems collaboratively over the course of the event.

- The Dark Patterns website (*https://darkpatterns.org*) has been instrumental in exposing the tricks that frustrate users into doing what businesses want them to do. Giving a name to something brings it into the light. This site's work in identifying these patterns helps shame companies who use them.

Inclusion

Bad design only works to serve the majority or the privileged few. Good design is inclusive and widens the bridge so that all can enjoy the benefits of technology. Here are some companies doing just that:

- Be My Eyes (*http://www.bemyeyes.org*) is an innovative app that is designed to help those with sight assist the blind when they need help on the go. It does this by quickly connecting a blind person's phone camera with a sighted person's device by sending them an alert. The sighted person then tells them what they need to know. The design of the app allows for ease of use and helps the blind live better lives, while enabling the people who want to help.

- Google (*https://www.google.com/accessibility*) does a lot to ensure its many products are accessible. Its accessibility standards serve as a great example of how to roll out accessibility over a variety of platforms, UIs, and apps and allow a much wider audience to access Google's technology.

- The BBC (*http://www.bbc.com*) has consistently been striving toward a more accessible website. It's an inspiration to many website designers. Not only does it look good, but it's accessible to the point where there is an accessible version of the onscreen keyboard in its children's games. The BBC also offers many how-to guides to help depending on the user's need for assistance (see Figure 8-1).

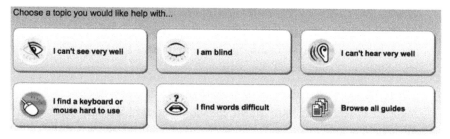

Choose a topic you would like help with...

I can't see very well   I am blind   I can't hear very well

I find a keyboard or mouse hard to use   I find words difficult   Browse all guides

FIGURE 8-1.
Screenshot from BBC My Web My Way. The BBC offers many guides that are useful to people who might need accessibility features.

Justice

The Digital Service is the design agency for the US government. Its goal is to redefine people's experience with their government. Talented designers are now tackling some of the government's most difficult design challenges, untangling bureaucracy and doing their best to promote user-centric design. Here are some other groups that are hard at work on behalf of those that need it most:

- 18F (*https://18f.gsa.gov*) is a team of top-notch designers, developers, and product specialists inside the General Services Administration. They make great products for the American people. Like the Digital Service, they are working hard to use technology and design to create better interactions between the government and its people in the US.

- Designers 4 Justice (*https://www.facebook.com/groups/designjustice*) is a group of over 1,500 volunteers amplifying nonprofit and justice-related causes through design.

- Open Source Design (*http://opensourcedesign.net*) is a community of designers and developers pushing for more open design processes and improving the user experience and interface design of open source software. They provide resources, put on events, and present talks targeted at developers and designers interested in working and designing in open source. They have a list of projects looking for designers to contribute.

What Will You Do?

We hope that in the course of this book we have been able to shine some light on some important issues in design, and also have lit a passion in your heart for change. Now it's your turn. You have the power to make a difference. What will you choose to do? How much effort are you willing to give? You can step up to the plate and join one of these fine organizations that are working to make a difference, support them, or start something of your own. The end of tragic design is in our hands, and a better-designed world for all starts with you.

Let's use design to make the world a better place.

Companies, Products, and Links

Throughout this book, we have discussed many examples that come from existing products and companies. We use these examples to illustrate important concepts and as a learning opportunity. If you are interested in learning more about any of these products or companies, here's a list, ordered alphabetically.

PRODUCT	COMPANY OR ORGANIZATION	LINK
18F	General Services Administration	*https://18f.gsa.gov*
Airbnb	Airbnb, Inc.	*https://www.airbnb.com*
Airbus A320	Airbus Group SE	*https://www.airbus.com*
Amazon.ca	Amazon.com, Inc.	*https://www.amazon.ca*
AOL	AOL Inc.	*http://my.xfinity.com*
Apple Mail	Apple Inc.	*http://www.apple.com*
Apple TV	Apple Inc.	*http://www.apple.com/apple-tv*
Articulating Design Decisions	O'Reilly Media, Inc.	*http://bit.ly/articulating-design-decisions*
BBC My Web My Way	BBC	*http://www.bbc.co.uk/accessibility*
Behance	Adobe	*https://www.behance.net*
California Prison Appointment Scheduing	California Department of Corrections and Rehabilitation	*http://visitorreservations.cdcr.ca.gov*
Center for Civic Design	Oxide Design Co.	*http://civicdesign.org*
Chrome Browser	Google Inc.	*https://www.google.com/chrome*

PRODUCT	COMPANY OR ORGANIZATION	LINK
Chrome for Android	Google Inc.	*www.google.ca/ chrome*
Cluster	Cluster Labs, Inc.	*https://cluster.co*
Code for America	Code for America Labs, Inc.	*https://www.codefo- ramerica.org*
Colorsafe	Donielle Berg and Adrian Rapp	*http://colorsafe.co*
Comcast	Comcast	*http://xfinity.com*
Dell	Dell	*http://www.dell.com*
Design in Tech Reports	Kleiner Perkins Caufield & Byers	*http://www.kpcb. com/blog/design-in- tech-report-2016*
Design with Intent	O'Reilly Media, Inc.	*http://oreil.ly/2o1w9I6*
Designer News	Tiny	*http://www.design- ernews.co*
Diablo	Blizzard Entertainment	*https://us.battle.net/ d3/en*
Dots	Playdots, Inc.	*https://www.dots.co*
Dribbble	Tiny	*https://dribbble.com*
eBay	eBay Inc	*http://www.ebay.com*
Epic	Epic Systems Corporation	*http://www.epic.com*
Facebook	Facebook Inc.	*https://www.face- book.com*
Facebook Messenger for iPhone	Facebook Inc.	*https://www.messen- ger.com*
Ford Pinto	Ford Motor Company	*http://www.ford.com*
Gmail	Google Inc.	*https://www.google. com/gmail*
Google Calendar	Google Inc.	*https://www.google. com/calendar*
Google Search	Google Inc.	*https://www.google. com*
Handy	Handy	*https://www.handy. com*

PRODUCT	COMPANY OR ORGANIZATION	LINK
Healthcare.gov	U.S. Centers for Medicare & Medicaid Services	*https://www.health-care.gov*
iOS on iPhone	Apple Inc.	*http://www.apple.com*
Iowa Department of Human Services	Iowa Department of Human Services	*https://dhsservices.iowa.gov*
iTunes	Apple Inc.	*http://www.apple.com/itunes*
Kellogg Canada Newsletter	Kellogg Company (Canada)	*http://www.kelloggs.ca*
LinkedIn	LinkedIn	*https://www.linkedin.com*
Mac App Store	Apple Inc.	*http://www.apple.com/osx/apps/app-store*
MailChimp	MailChimp	*https://mailchimp.com*
Medium	Medium Corporation	*https://medium.com*
Microsoft Office Assistant	Microsoft Corporation	*https://www.microsoft.com/en-us/windows/get-windows-10*
Microsoft Windows 10	Microsoft Corporation	*https://www.microsoft.com/en-us/windows/get-windows-10*
MyAlabama	State of Alabama	*https://www.myalabama.gov/services*
Nebraska Department of Health & Human Services	Nebraska Department of Health & Human Services	*http://bit.ly/2n5asuE*
Negative Underwear	Negative Underwear	*https://negativeunderwear.com*
Nightscout project	James Wedding	*http://www.nightscout.info*
OSX	Apple Inc.	*http://www.apple.com*
Porter Airline Newsletter	Porter Airlines	*https://www.flyporter.com*

PRODUCT	COMPANY OR ORGANIZATION	LINK
QuickBooks	Intuit Inc.	*https://quickbooks.intuit.com*
Rogers Wireless Newsletter	Rogers Wireless	*http://www.rogers.com*
Royal Mail	Royal Mail plc	*http://www.royalmail.com*
Scana Propulsion (Ferry)	Scana Propulsion	*http://scanapropulsion.com/about*
SEAT Mii	SEAT	*http://www.seat.com/carworlds/mii/mii-by-cosmopolitan.html*
Sendspace	Sendspace	*https://www.sendspace.com*
Shopify	Shopify Inc.	*https://www.shopify.com*
Slack	Slack	*https://slack.com*
Smashing Magazine	Vitaly Friedman and Sven Lennartz	*https://www.smashingmagazine.com*
Supplemental Nutrition Assistance Program (SNAP)	USA	*http://bit.ly/2ov3vTL*
Tesla Model S	Tesla Motors	*https://www.tesla.com/models*
The Open Design Foundation	Garth Braithwaite	*http://opendesign.foundation*
Therac-25	Atomic Energy of Canada Limited (AECL)	*http://www.aecl.ca/en/home/default.aspx*
To Park or Not to Park	Nikki Sylianteng	*http://toparkornotto-park.com*
Tragic Design Website	Jonathan Shariat & Cynthia Savard Saucier	*http://www.tragicde-sign.com*
Tumblr	Tumblr, Inc	*https://www.tumblr.com*
Twinject	Amedra Pharmaceuticals LLC	*http://www.twinject.com*

PRODUCT	COMPANY OR ORGANIZATION	LINK
Twitter	Twitter Inc.	*https://twitter.com*
U-Haul	U-Haul	*https://www.uhaul.com*
UX Booth	UX Booth	*http://www.uxbooth.com*
UX Magazine	UX Magazine	*http://uxmag.com*
WordPress	WordPress Foundation	*https://wordpress.org*
Xbox	Microsoft Corporation	*http://www.xbox.com*

[*Index*]

interview with Amy Cueva, 10–16
success stories, 183–184
Swiss Cheese model of accident
    causation, 3–4
Therac-25 case study, 19–28
hearing impairment, 119
Hecquet, Christian, 38–41
Hemingway Editor tool, 124
Hersman, Deborah A. P., 28
hidden costs, understanding and
    identifying, 7–9, 79
hierarchy of needs (customers), 15–
    16
hostile architecture, 128
human-centered design. *See* user-
    centered design (UCD)
human-computer interaction
    (HCI), 54
human right, internet access
    as, 127–128
humiliation, design causing harm
    through, 90–91
hyperlinks, providing context
    for, 124

I

IDEO design company, 184
IEC 61025 (Fault Tree Analysis), 47–
    48
IEC 62304 (Medical Device Soft-
    ware), 27
IEC 62366:2007 (Use Error
    Chart), 18–19
images on websites
    alt text for, 123
    avoiding carousels/sliders, 124–
        125
    embedded text in, 124
impolite technologies
    about, 55
    as attention freaks, 60–62
    as gluttons, 59–60
    as lazy, 57–59
    Microsoft Office Assistant case
        study, 60–62
    polite technologies compared
        to, 62–68
    as selfish, 55–56
inadvertent cruelty of edge cases, 86–
    89, 106–107
inclusive design, 128–135

industrial design. *See* product design
injuries, minor versus serious, 28–29
injustice concept
    about, 135
    Food Stamp program, 135–139
    parking tickets, 139–141
    presidential elections, 144–148
    prison visiting, 142–145
    success stories for justice, 186
intended actions (Use Error
    Chart), 18–19
interface design
    10 Usability Heuristics for Inter-
        face Design, 21–25, 30
    interface that killed Jenny, 1–3
    interview with Maya Benari
        on, 110
    modes in, 41–42
    of open source software, 186
    Swiss Cheese model in, 3–4
International Council of Design, 6
International Electrotechnical Com-
    mission (IEC)
    IEC 61025 standard, 47–48
    life cycle development stan-
        dard, 27
internet access, 127–129
interviews
    with Aaron Sklar, 50–52
    with Amy Cueva, 10–16
    with Dean Hamack, 150–152
    with Garth Braithwaite, 82–83
    with Maya Benari, 109–114
intuitive design to access technol-
    ogy, 116–117
iPad (Apple), 117–118
iPhone (Apple)
    apps using back-and-switch dark
        patterns, 69
    Facebook Messenger permission
        dialog, 57
    home screen dancing mode, 30
    intuitive design to access technol-
        ogy, 116
iPod (Apple), 49
iTunes media library (Apple)
    iPhone apps using back-and-
        switch dark patterns, 69
    silent downloads and, 59–60

physical disabilities, 119
Plain Language Action and Information Network (PLAIN), 124
Plutchik, Robert, 159
Plutchik's wheel, 159–160
polite technologies compared to impolite technologies, 62–68
Porter airline, 78
power user features
  about, 90
  making settings understandable, 91–93
  options no one understands, 92–93
  shortcut considerations, 90–91
Prescribe Design movement, 51, 183–184
presidential elections, 144–148
Presidential Innovation Fellowship, 111
prioritizing
  feature development, 100–101
  roads for snow removal, 131
prison visiting, communicating effectively, 142–145
product design. See also accessibility
  changing testing scenarios, 103–104
  designing for failure, 104–105
  designing safeguards, 8–9, 93–95
  Ford Pinto case study, 32–38
  handling user deaths, 98–100
  importance of error states, 106–107
  life cycle development standard, 27
  organizing catastrophic brainstorms, 102–103
  power of symbols, 96–98
  recognizing changes in emotional state versus database state, 95
  reprioritizing feature development, 100–101
  Sheriff role rotation in, 100–101
  success stories, 183–187
  understanding and identifying hidden costs, 7–9
prototyping
  interview with Aaron Sklar on, 51–52

interview with Maya Benari on, 111, 112
  usage suggestions, 178

Q

qualitative data, 17, 85, 156–157
quantitative data, 17, 85, 155–157
quasimodes, 41–42
queries for pain points, 154
QuickBooks online settings page, 64

R

radiation therapy case study, 19–28
Raskin, Jef, 41
reciprocity technique, 73
Reeve, Christopher, 127
Registered Graphic Designers (RGD), 126–127
Rehabilitation Act (1973), 170
Righi, Carol, 176
roach-motels dark pattern, 75
road accidents, diversity-conscious design and, 132–134
Rock Health venture group, 184
Rogers Media (company), 78
roles and responsibilities of designers
  about, 5–6
  client paradox, 5–6
  Sad Sheriff, 100–101
  suggested actions for designers, 169–181
  understanding and identifying hidden costs, 7–9
Root Cause Analysis (RCA), 48
Royal Mail newsletter registration form, 76–77

S

sadden, design can. See design can sadden
Sad Sheriff, 100–101
safeguards for product design, 8–9, 93–95, 101–102
scope creep, 8
screen readers, 128
search engine optimization (SEO), 119
search feature in applications, 90–91
search queries for pain points, 154

About the Authors

Jonathan Shariat is a thoughtful designer with a big heart for designing things that matter. He brings to the table eight years of experience designing in healthcare, file sharing, and publishing. He has worked for himself, for startups, and for large companies as well.

Jonathan didn't always know he would be a designer. He first started out in high school pursuing animation. However, as he sat down to choose a path for college, he drew a Venn diagram. One circle for the things he was good at. Another for the things he enjoyed. A third for jobs that had demand and a good future. Through this process he discovered user interface design: a path that utilized both his creative side and his analytical side. He attended the Art Institute of California, where he studied design and web development, and received the Outstanding Student Achievement Award for his work there.

Jonathan has helped build apps that are used by over 30 million people at YouSendIt (now called Hightail) and aided startups as a freelancer to kick their experiences into high gear. He also was the Director of Product at Therapydia, where he helped create a better connection between physical therapists and their patients. He is currently a Senior Interaction Designer at Intuit in Mountain View, CA.

Jonathan believes the best way to learn is to turn around and teach someone. Writing has been an avenue to do just that, and to document his journey in design. Today Jonathan is continuing to explore the topic of this book through his newsletter (*http://tragicdesign.com*). He also has a popular Twitter account (@DesignUXUI) where he shares things he is thinking about and learning, as well as humorous GIFs and anecdotes. He gives talks about design around the world and enjoys mentoring young designers.

Cynthia Savard Saucier is a user experience designer interested in behavioral psychology, accessibility, and people management. When not at work, you'll find her making chocolates in her kitchen or obsessively listening to podcasts. She is also the proud mother of a little one and wishes that he will grow up in a world where you don't need a label to know if you must push (or pull) a door.

In high school, Cynthia first saw a television remote control with oversized buttons at a friend's house. Her mom was an occupational therapist helping people with visual impairments. It was her first introduction to a field that would later become her passion. She pursued industrial design at the University of Montréal, and realized that interface design was as potent as product design. Her final project, for which she received awards, was aimed at bridging the gap between grandparents and children. It definitely cemented her interest in the user experience field.

Cynthia started her career in an agency specializing in user experience and user tests, working on government websites, television networks, and public transit websites. She then joined a digital agency, leading the team of designers, and more recently joined Shopify, a large Canadian company, where she is Director of Design.

On top of her daytime job, Cynthia mentors startups and is regularly invited to speak at events around the world, where her playful approach both startles and charms. In her conferences, she shares her passion and her point of view: user-centered design is a reality, not a utopian methodology. Follow her on Twitter (@CynthiaSavard) to read her complaints to companies using dark patterns.

Colophon

The animal on the cover of *Tragic Design* is a Portuguese man-o-war jellyfish.

The cover image is a color illustration by Karen Montgomery, based on a black and white engraving from *Tenney*. The cover fonts are URW Typewriter and Guardian Sans. The text font is Scala; and the heading font is Gotham.

Have it your way.

Milton Keynes UK
Ingram Content Group UK Ltd.
UKHW020658040824
446500UK00011B/36